. . . I remember pumping his chest anc
eye the fire trucks pull up.

HURRY . . . PLEASE HURRY

WHY WERE THEY WALKING . . . RUN!

Then, suddenly, they were there, pulling me off my son, my husband running into the room. It's true what they say about things slowing down. I felt a thick fog surrounding me, forcing everything to slow: the firemen pulling out the stretcher, my husband covering his mouth with his hand as he looked down at our son . . . MY SON. I knew. I knew he was gone. I had felt his last breath leave him with a rasp then gurgle as I tried desperately to breathe life back into him over and over again. I started pushing through the men in the room, not knowing where I was running to. I could hear someone screaming. I could feel the bile rising in my throat. Then I realized the screaming was coming from me. I opened my eyes and found I was lying on my son's bed, curled up in his pillow and comforter, screaming. I remember seeing his shoes on the floor, his shoes that will never be worn again.

Grabbing the comforter, I somehow stumbled into the twins' room, where Brian had the tiny babies.

OH MY GOD . . . OH MY GOD . . .

They have lost their brother. I no longer have four boys.

I looked down at my hands as I crouched on the floor next to the three boys, my hands sticking to Jason's comforter. Sticking because his blood was drying on my hands. I was losing it, things were going dark. I can't do this. I CAN'T DO THIS! Brian grabbed my hand I was watching the blood dry on, all but fourteen years old, looked right into my wild eyes, and said, "Don't do it, Mom, don't do anything stupid."

I began to vomit. I was completely and utterly overcome.

* * *

This was not the grief I had felt with previous losses. This was a dark, thick mass bubbling up from deep inside my gut—and it burned. Like oil to a flame, that mass burned hot and without let up. It burned until I was on fire . . . every second of every day

~ Kimberly Tocco

What does it all mean? Why? What is the meaning of this life?

Well, darling, that is where life becomes an adventure . . . in the search for it.

~ Tenacious T

It is not what you go through, it's how you come through it.

~ Kimberly Tocco (aka, Tenacious T)

* * *

Overcome

Memoirs of a Suicide

Kimberly Tocco

Disclaimer:

The author strives to be as accurate and complete as possible in the creation of this book, notwithstanding the fact that the author does not warrant or represent at any time that the contents within are accurate due to the rapidly changing nature of the Internet.

While all attempts have been made to verify information provided in this publication, the Author and Publisher assume no responsibility and are not liable for errors, omissions, or contrary interpretation of the subject matter herein. The Author and Publisher hereby disclaim any liability, loss or damage incurred as a result of the application and utilization, whether directly or indirectly, of any information, suggestion, advice, or procedure in this book. Any perceived slights of specific persons, peoples, or organizations are unintentional.

Printed in the United States of America

Jones Media Publishing
www.jonesmediapublishing.com

ISBN: 978-1-945849-95-4 paperback
JMP2020.4

Dedication

To my husband, who has given me his all, held me, cared for me, and learned to say "Fuck Yeah!" with every crazy idea. I owe you. You can rest now, it's time for your abundance. You have been such a gift to me. I am so in love with you.

Brian, my first born, the one who has been with me longer than any other. I know your childhood wasn't easy, full of loss and trauma. Yet, not unlike your mother, you held strong to who you are, and of you I am so proud.

My twins, Joey and Petey, my little tenacious ones. You are the sweet souls who reminded me to hold on and to nurture the little girl in me. Teaching me joy and to step back from work just a little bit so I don't miss out on the gift of your laughter.

Jacob Drozdowicz, for taking care of his first base glove, I will forever be grateful.

Ben Drozdowicz, you played with his glove in your final championship game . . . and gave me the medal. What a gift!

Peter and Andrea Drozdowicz, you have always been there for us and we are so thankful for you and your family.

To all of Jason's friends who held us in your arms as we sobbed together, you saved my sanity.

Jonathan Hilton, for being my best friend.

Joe Buzzello. Thank you, Yoda. This jedi is forever thankful.

Brian Culhane, The Success Philosopher. Thank you for showing me the path to Pain Freedom.

Russell Shaw. For the gift of modern classical music, much needed during the final push on the book.

Juma Entertainment, for choosing me to be on national television, Jason is dancing!

Brad Pickett, for giving me the courage to "see."

Jason Paul Legere

Everything I do is a dedication to you. I miss you beyond words.

Contents

Author's Preface

There are so many stories of inspiration, heroism, survivors, and how they overcame seemingly impossible situations. Humankind's greatest altruism and achievements have been born from our deepest sorrows.

In *Good Will Hunting*, Robin Williams's character Sean said, "You don't know about real loss, 'cause it only occurs when you've loved something more than yourself."

We have faith, those who have been ground down into dust only to be stepped on again and again. That's what an angel is, the light inside us all, unlocked through suffering, unlocked so we can make a difference.

That's what this book is for me. My greatest achievements have always been my children. This book is my Jason. He isn't here to show you what kind of light he was meant to be, so I am doing that for him.

* * *

Everything you are about to read is true, unfiltered, and raw. Some of this content may offend or shock, but most of it should ignite a fire inside you and leave you forever changed. We are all but leaves on the same tree, and our stories are the whispers that blow through them. I couldn't tell it any other way.

* * *

Chapter 1: He is Dead

"Boys! Breakfast!"

Every morning I would make breakfast for my two older boys, Brian, 14, and Jason, 13. Those two were only twelve months apart and in the same grade. Almost like twins, really, they were so close. Ironically, I ended up having twins eleven years after Jason was born, pudgy little dudes named Joey and Petey. They were watching cartoons and playing with toys to the side of the kitchen as I finished up cooking.

"Boys!" *Jesus, how many times do I need to say that?*

Down came Brian, a handsome, dark-haired kid with brilliant hazel eyes. I had made English muffins with egg and cheese, a healthy version of the fast food item. I had been trying to get the boys to eat a better breakfast. Neither of them likes breakfast sandwiches, and Brian rolled his eyes, sat down, and started picking at it.

"Mom, you know I hate these!" Jason whined as I looked up from Brian. Jason was a beautiful young man. Six foot one with dark blond hair and the clearest color of green eyes I have ever seen.

"I do not want to hear it! We need to hustle. I have been calling you guys, and when you finally get down here, you won't eat. JUST EAT IT!" My temper was getting to me. I was tired and just wanted a "thank you for cooking, Mom."

Just then, my husband, Pete, came down the stairs. He was dressed for a union meeting, an extra position he took so he could support his fire department.

"Just do as your mother asks, Jason."

Jason stood up from the table and knocked the chair to the floor. I had never seen him like this. Never. The hair on the back of my neck was raised, everything in the air was charged, and Jason stood face to face with my husband. I could see the two of them exchanging words, but I couldn't hear it, or I do not recall. I only remember something really off about the entire situation.

"Get upstairs! You are not going to school like this and you need to wait until I get back from these meetings. Brian, finish getting ready and help your mom put the twins in the car and she will take you to school." Pete walked over, kissed me on the cheek, and said in my ear, "Don't let him go to school, I will talk to him when I get back." With that he left out the front door. I sat down at the table, Brian on the floor with the twins, and Jason standing in the hallway between the kitchen and the stairs.

"I hate you!" Jason said to me, and I looked up at him. I didn't know what to say. I was hurt from trying so hard to cook, then the anger he expressed toward us, and now he tells me he hates me. I felt like I didn't recognize him. He had such a dark look on his face. "Yeah, well, I hate you too. Just go upstairs and we will talk when Dad gets back," I frustratingly stated.

"Hello?" My phone was ringing.

"How is he?" It was Pete calling from the car.

"I don't know. I just sent him upstairs. He told me he hates me . . . Ugh. And I said it back," I told him, feeling very childish.

"He will be fine. Tell him to pick up his phone, I want to talk to him."

"Jason, pick up your phone when Dad calls!" I yelled upstairs to him.

A few minutes later my phone rings again. "Hello?"

"What is he doing now?" Pete asked me.

Just then I heard a noise.

"Ah, yeah, sounds like he just threw something. How was he when you spoke with him?"

Jason, being a baseball player, was always throwing things, happy or mad.

"I just tried to explain to him that he does not get to make all his own choices. He just kept asking me why he had to eat something he didn't want to and why he couldn't play video games when he wanted and stuff like that. I told him we love him but that's just not how things work. We are his parents, and it's our job to raise him, and he has to follow the rules."

This was a very common discussion in our house. Having two teenage boys, we had a few rules to follow. Video games on weekends only, homework first before friends, pick up your rooms . . . the usual suspects. What was so odd about it on this day was that Jason was really having a hard time with it, with the rules. He had always been the one to offer help and go the extra mile. He would complain, of course, but this . . . he was more than angry, he was off.

"He is not picking up his phone and I wasn't done talking to him. Call him down so he can talk to me on this phone."

"Jason!" I yelled.

Nothing.

"Jason . . . Oh, never mind, I will bring the phone upstairs with me," I said as I started for the stairs. "Jason! He isn't answering. Brian come help me find your brother. Jason!"

I was going from room to room, first his room, not there, Brian's room, twins' room. I felt Brian behind me as I headed into my room. My heart was pounding. Something was wrong. "I can't find him, I can't . . ."

As soon as I stepped into my closet, I could smell gun powder.

"Oh my God! OH MY GOD, I SMELL GUN POWDER . . . I smell it!"

My eyes were dodging rapidly between the couple of rifles and BB gun. "JAAASON!! He is not in the closet: where is he, where is he?"

I was panicking.

"The ammunition is in the safe, those are not loaded. Check the ammunition," Peter said over the phone.

"I found him, Mom! He is over here. MOM!" Brian screamed.

I looked over in the direction he was pointing.

My room was set up in such a way that when you enter the master you are looking at the east wall, which the headboard of my massive bed sat against, and the closet and bath to the south. As you walk out of the master bath, you look toward the north wall, and there on the floor at the foot of the bed you could see Jason's feet, the rest of him hidden by the bed, my side of the bed, where I had hidden the only loaded gun in the house, a lightweight, hair-trigger Ruger .38 revolver.

"His feet, do you see them?" Brian asked

My head was spinning.

"Grab the twins, take them to their room, do not let them see this. Stay there," I instructed with a voice stronger than I knew I was at that moment, all while I ran to that side of the bed.

Nothing prepares you for something like this. I still had the phone to my ear, my husband I think saying he was turning around . . . and then I saw him.

"HHHEEEE IS DEAD! OH, GOD, NO . . . he . . . he is dead!" I remember screaming into the phone at the same time Pete was screaming to call 911.

I had a landline phone in my hand and I immediately looked back down to hang up and dialed 911.

But what I had seen was branded on my eyes. He was half on his side, half on his back, my gun was there on the floor. His beautiful mouth slightly open, and as my eyes traveled up, I saw the dark hole, his eyes black.

Towel . . . Grab a towel and wrap his head in it, apply pressure. NOW! This was my own voice in my head while I dialed 911. I ran to the bathroom, grabbed a towel, and put the phone on speaker.

"911, what is your emergency?"

I could not tell you if it was a male or female. All I could think was HURRY!

"My son, he has shot himself. I need an ambulance now! My address is twenty-nine twenty-one East Pillar Drive. Please hurry!"

"Slow down, ma'am, I can't understand you. What is your emergency?"

"He's dead, he's dead, he's dead . . . please hurry!"

I had wrapped the top of his head as tight as I could with the towel, covering his eyes and the wound. I was trying to lay him flat so I could start compressions.

"He is heavy. Oh, GOD, I can't get him on his back. PLEASE HELP ME!"

Just then his body slid enough so I could put him on his back . . . and I saw his mouth open. He was breathing! I started compressions and mouth to mouth.

"One, two, three. How many do I do again? HOW MANY?" I was screaming to the 911 operator.

I knew it was thirty, but it felt so long to go between breaths into his mouth. I do not know what they replied, I just kept going. I am not sure how many minutes went by, but I knew they were too late.

As I continued, I felt him die.

I pushed my breath into his body, and unlike the first few times, this time my breath came right back out . . . like a balloon deflating.

I felt his body let go.

Chapter 2: Aftermath

NO, no, don't let go. NO!

"Jason, I love you. Oh, my boy, why? WHY?"

I kept pushing my lungs into his, but it just gurgled out.

I remember pumping his chest and seeing through the corner of my eye the fire trucks pull up.

HURRY . . . PLEASE HURRY

WHY WERE THEY WALKING? RUN!

Then, suddenly, they were there, pulling me off my son, my husband running into the room. It's true what they say about things slowing down. I felt a thick fog surrounding me, forcing everything to slow. The firemen pulling out the stretcher, my husband covering his mouth with his hand as he looked down at our son. MY SON.

I knew. I knew he was gone.

I had felt his last breath leave him with a rasp then gurgle as I had tried desperately to breathe life back into him over and over again. I started pushing through the men in the room, not knowing where I was running to. I could hear someone was screaming. I could feel the bile rising in my throat. Then I realized the screaming was coming from me. I opened my eyes and found I was lying on his bed, curled up in his pillow and comforter. Screaming. I remember seeing his shoes on the floor, his shoes that will never be worn again.

Grabbing the comforter, I somehow stumbled into the twins' room where Brian had the three-year-olds.

OH MY GOD . . . OH MY GOD.

THEY HAVE LOST THEIR BROTHER. I NO LONGER HAVE FOUR BOYS.

HE IS DEAD.

I looked down at my hands as I crouched to the floor next to the three boys, my hands sticking to Jason's comforter.

Sticking because his blood was drying on my hands.

I was losing it. Things were going dark.

I can't do this. I CAN'T DO THIS.

Brian grabbed my hand I was watching the blood dry on. All but fourteen years old, he looked right into my wild eyes and said, "Don't do it, Mom. Don't do anything stupid."

I knew he could see it, that I was going to shut down, that I wanted to run. I stood up while he held my hand, and as Pete and an officer headed our way, I could see the worry on the officer's face, and I heard my husband whisper, "Just tell her we have something, just tell her that."

I heard what he said. I understood he thought that would keep me calm, thinking he was giving me hope. Hope is an expectation based on desire, and in that moment, Pete new that's all he could give me.

"Please, please, please, I will take him no matter what condition. Please tell me you have something, PLEASE. I can take care of him, just give him back to me."

"Yes, ma'am, yes, we, ah, we are still working. We are going to take him by ambulance now," he stated, not able to look in my eyes.

I began to vomit. I was completely and utterly overcome.

I remember looking up from the toilet. I will never ever forget looking up and seeing his window just above his tank. I was in HIS bathroom. I could hear the crew go by, carrying my son's lifeless body down the stairs. I listened for the sirens, not knowing what to do. The hospital, he is at the hospital, you need to get up.

GET UP!

It was really hard to stand. Brian was there, and somehow we ended up downstairs, where I started throwing up again. There was a phone in my face. My husband's mother, crying.

People were around me, helping me into a car. I can hear what they are saying, but it's like I am underwater.

I can only see Jason, his body reflexing, that last breath leaving him. Walking down a white hall . . . This isn't where I want him, no, no, why is he here? They are taking me into a room. "Stop . . . STOP!"

I planted my feet. I couldn't go in there. Not like this, not in the bright hospital lights. I couldn't see those black eyes again.

"Please take a towel and cover . . . cover the . . ." I could not say hole, but they understood.

He lay there, my beautiful boy, bags on his hands, body covered in a sheet, his shirt off.

I slowly looked up to his face, his mouth and nose, the rest covered in a towel. Someone was sitting me down, and my husband asked if his wife could hold her son's hand. They removed the bag from his left hand, the side I was sitting on, and Pete put my hand inside Jason's

I wept. A deep, dark cry of sorrow. I knew in that moment, everything I was, everything I had built up to be in my entire life was shattered beyond repair. There was no coming back from this. That girl lays dead with her son on the table in front of her.

Brian was not in there with us. He did not need to see his brother like this. They needed me to be in the other room with him, and like a robot I went over to the cold white round tables you see in every hospital. Not really something you give thought to until you are sitting at one discussing your sons final arrangements.

Brian was next to me, sitting up strong, holding my hand. He had never been like this. He was not the affectionate type, and he was closer to Jason than anyone. Yet, here he sat, looking at me like I was going to break. Brian had been difficult, struggling with challenging behaviors and acting out at school. For the longest time, therapists thought it was the aftermath from the trauma he went through as a toddler. His biological father was bipolar and I had been abused in front of the boys. He had been doing much better for a couple of years, but it was Jason who seemed more like the older brother.

Jason, at age two, was the same height as his brother, and by thirteen he was 6'1". He had all the charm of his father but the kind heart of his mother. Jason loved his brother more than anything, and they stood up for each other. They had never been apart, excepting a night here and there. Same grade, same friends . . . for all intents and purposes, they were twins.

Where my soul had been ripped from my body, Brian's heart had followed with the death of his brother. Yet, there he sat holding my hand, brave and strong. Some might even say his brother threw him some mojo that day . . . and for many days to follow. Looking at him in that moment, something stirred enough to remember that maybe Jason could throw "life" as well.

"We need to donate his organs." My voice was very raw, it was hard to speak. "His organs, we can save someone's life. My Jason was healthy and strong."

That was a difficult decision, but something in me said, *Yes, he would want that.* Again, the fog came over like a thick syrup, moving slowly. I answered some questions on the phone, asking about his bones and tissues. "Yes, yes, take those."

I was starting to break again, and I realized we had left the hospital.

"NO, NO, don't take me back there. I can't go back, ever, don't go back." In a panic, I looked for my husband.

"No, we are going to my mom's. You do not have to go back there. Mom has the twins."

People coming in, sitting in a chair, my face wet. *What is happening?* I could not accept the new reality. This is not how it's supposed to be. *How is he gone? Why can't we fix it? There has to be a way.*

As night fell, I found myself sitting on the floor in Pete's mom's house, still crying. It was about one o'clock in the morning, and the world was quiet. I looked over to my husband and asked him, "Is this what you meant when you said there are worse things that can happen?"

Pete, as I mentioned before, was the gift life gave me. When I was scared and tired of the battles to keep my kids safe and away from their father, he was there to give me strength. When my sister passed and father shortly after, he was there to hold me gently and help me grieve. When I was going through IVF to conceive the twins, even when one of the twins was found to have autism, he always said, "It's OK, there are worse things that can happen, we can get through this as long as we have each other."

In this moment, over all others, I needed him to be my light. I needed him to somehow look at me and say, "It's OK, there are worse things that can happen. Everything has a way of working itself out."

"Is this it? Is this what you meant?"

When Pete looked up from the side of the bed my heart sank. I had never seen him this way. He had been crying, which I had only seen on one other occasion—when his father died. But even then, it was not like this. It was as if for the first time he did not have the strength to hold in that kind of pain.

He replied, "Yes, this is what I meant. There is nothing worse than this." He began to weep.

And like that last breath I felt leave my son's body, I knew there was no coming back.

Chapter 3: Denial

Memoir I

Denial: the action of declaring something to be untrue. "She shook her head in denial."

May 2011

I'M BAAAACK!

Yes, that's right, after a long hiatus I have returned to my love of writing. Usually I write in a humorous "historical fiction" style, taking daily events I experience and turning them into an overexaggerated version of what happened. I will return to that in short, but this particular post will be a very real and sober telling of living without my child.

Most of you know I lost my beautiful boy a couple of months ago. For those that don't, I lost him suddenly and unexpectedly to a preventable firearms accident at the age of thirteen. I always used to hear the stories of children playing with guns and to keep your firearms locked up and unloaded.

"That will never happen to me" was always my first response, especially since my children had become older.

Yet, older does not mean educated in the handling of firearms. Older does not mean invulnerable to the temptations of handling a gun even when they are told of the dangers. Older does not mean you can keep one gun loaded for protection. Needless to say, I have learned that lesson, and learned it hard. Many of my friends have asked, "How do you do it? How do you go on?"

There is no easy answer to this question. There is no easy way to keep a smile on your face or stuff the extreme emotions down long enough to get you through any given moment. For me, it's like I have been buried alive. I feel the weight of his loss as six feet of dirt covering my body; the heavy soil crushing my soul. I feel the wind knocked out of me every time I picture his face, like the diminishing air that goes with being buried under the ground. The hole in my heart eats away at me like the little creatures in the soil gorging on your body.

Yet, somehow, I slowly dig my way up, climb to the surface, put my gloves on and FIGHT through another day. I say FIGHT because it is a battle to surface and a battle to breathe. I long to end my pain and hold my boy in Heaven, talk to him again. What would that make me? It would make me a coward and a person that not only abandoned her family but caused the intense pain I am feeling to everyone I love.

Yes, I cry and scream, I drink too much wine, and I yell at my husband. I also hold onto to him, to my friends and family, to the knowledge that each day I am making Jason proud.

I go on because I have no right to do otherwise. No right to hurt those who have stood by me and no right to make Jason's loss completely senseless. I am here to bring my son's memory of love, compassion, and strength to all I know and to his charity, JPL: (Jason's Propulsion League) sponsoring underprivileged children by paying for the fees and equipment so they can play baseball. It's what he would have wanted, something I know he is helping me with.

And through these small efforts, getting out of bed, eating, taking care of his brothers, I keep him with me, and that brings a smile to my face!

* * *

TODAY

I was in denial, in "blame mode." I was dying inside. After that first night, memories come in fog-riddled waves. Like I was sitting, crouched down with my arms over my head in the middle of a hot, red tornado. An angry red funnel of clouds and black dirt spinning so fast I cannot hear, and I am too scared to look up. I just want to sit here and let it all just get swept away.

GO AWAY!

But the world did not go away, and I had to pull my head out of my ass to bury my child.

He left me on a Tuesday, and by Saturday we were saying our final goodbyes. As I sat in my tornado, I would reach out just long enough to get the things done for my child that he deserved: a stunning collage of all our memories together, wrist bands ordered for the entire school and extended friends through baseball and grade school, flowers, food, and what to bury my son in.

That broke me even further. What will he wear for the next two hundred years down in the dark, cold ground? That does something very strange in your mind: it creates an irrational fear that somehow your child is still aware. I liken it to someone who has lost a limb. For a very long time they "feel" it, known as a "phantom limb." It's exactly that when you lose a child. Your brain, your mind, your soul cannot process it. He was still there, and I could not put my son in the ground. I remember I decided his last baseball uniform. His best year and favorite team he had played with.

"OK, now put this on your hand. Like that, yes! Now stand right there and Mommy is going to lightly toss the ball to you. Ready?" I gently taught Jason.

He was two years old, we were at my parents' house, and I had taken him outside in the front driveway to help him use his first baseball glove. I was working three jobs at this time. I had been on my own for a year after leaving their father and winning custody of both my boys and after a solid restraining order while awaiting final conviction. I was still working on final divorce papers to come through, but I had made significant progress and we were safe. I had bought a tiny plastic baseball glove and ball for him. Jason had incredible hand-eye coordination, even early on, and by the time he was two he was as tall as his three-year-old brother. I tossed the ball and he caught it. A bit in shock, I tried it again, further back. Again, he caught it.

This was the beginning of an incredible journey with my son that ended way too soon.

As Jason continued to grow and flourish, so did his talent. I practiced with him as often as I could and went to every game. I was the crazy mom who screamed in the bleachers and tried to be a co-coach. Jason could catch, Jason could hit, but his throwing arm was money. He quickly became the star, playing first base and pitching. At eleven years old, just shy of his twelfth birthday, he was clocked throwing eighty miles per hour.

Picture this: you are at a game for eleven and unders, your kid's team is up to bat, and out comes a six-foot-tall man-child who is throwing the ball eighty miles per hour. You can bet your ass I had a few parents asking for a birth certificate. We never had his speed tested again. We missed that opportunity. But in his last game, just two days before he took his life, he pitched a no-hitter.

Six-foot-one, strong, and focused. He had had several no-hitters in the last year.

I remember being very distracted because I had the twins and the game was on a Sunday night, thinking, Why didn't you bring your camera?

I never did take one video of my son pitching. Not one. I always thought I would have time, always thought he was going to make it to the big leagues . . .

So very many things I had thought I would see him do.

So, for his love of baseball, even for when he hated it, his life was filled with it, and I had a feeling he would want to leave us in his favorite jersey with his favorite number, thirteen.

Friday, we had planned a Rosary to be said with my son. I had not seen him since the hospital. Since before they, they . . .

I couldn't think about it, what they do to prepare the body, what they do when they save life with his precious organs . . .

Will I see the hole in his head?

The tornado was getting louder, cutting me off from what my mind could not handle.

"Kimberly, are you ready? Do you want to go in first?" It was Pete. He looked gray

"Yes, yes. How does he look?" I was scared, terrified I would see the black, open eyes.

I do not recall what was said after that. I was walking down an aisle, sickeningly long, yet in a small room with bench seating. Pete was holding onto me.

OH GOD, OH GOD.

Then I was there, by his side. He looked beautiful.

They had done an incredible job covering the wound. I could see the single entry point, which I had not the mindset to look for before.

Clean, right in the center.

I stopped looking. I went to his hair, the deep color of fresh sand on the beach in the morning. The perfect line of his nose to the point of his strong chin. He was a beautiful young man. I let go of my husband's hands and placed them on Jason's chest, shoulders, then his hands. I knew this would be the last time I ever see my son, the last time I would touch him, and I wanted to remember every last hair on his head. I began to sob and shake.

I didn't know how I was going to do this.

Just then a car horn started going off, an alarm, but just the horn. It kept going and going, and Pete and I began to laugh. We kind of joked that it was Jason telling me not to cry. Just then it stopped.

We laughed again, and I said, "OK, Jason, if that's you, I will never yell at your brothers ever again if you make a honk now."

Low and behold, a car honked as it went by the funeral hall. This is that phantom pain I was talking about, the way the mind looks for things that could be your child. I was to experience quite a lot of this to come.

"I want to be alone with him, please." I suddenly felt I needed it to be just him and me. Like the days past, just me and my boys.

"Are you sure?" Pete asked, taken aback.

"Yes, I need to be alone with him."

I never looked away from my boy as the doors closed behind me. I told him how much I loved him, how sorry I was, how if he could just please come back, PLEASE. I then laid my head on his chest. I had to find a way to walk out and let the Rosary service begin.

You see, I had asked they close his casket before anyone else comes in. I did not want them to see the hole. It was an accident, not on purpose, an accident, but they will think otherwise if they see that. If they see that, they will think he committed suicide. They will see my son differently, see us differently.

DENIAL

I was not accepting at this point the cold, hard truth, and the stigma that surrounds the word suicide was a fear that sat in waiting just at the base of my throat. I could not accept my Jason did not want to be here anymore. Because if I did, that meant I missed something, and it was my fault.

The night before the Rosary, at least I think it was the night before, Pete and a friend had put me in a car, and it was raining. It was a strange sensation, because I was perfectly aware we were going to see a therapist, that everyone was saying I was going to crack. Yet, how I processed it was as if I was standing off in the distance, watching it, like a movie I was trapped inside of. When we arrived at the destination, I recall Pete right next to me. He rarely left my side. We walked into a dark room with a young woman setting brochures down on the table. When I sat down, I picked up the material and immediately dropped it as if it were on fire.

It was a brochure about being a suicide survivor.

"Our son did not commit suicide, we don't know that. It was an accident. Why would you put those brochures down like that? It's only been two days!"

I was torn in half with what felt like a hot poker. I knew he had done this thing I refused to say. I knew he went upstairs with a state of mind I had never experienced with him before. I knew, but I also FELT, he regretted it, that it was not what he intended to do with that day or his life. Yet, here we were, and there that word was . . . suicide.

I didn't want people to think of him in that way. I did not want THAT to be how he was remembered, because my boy was much more than a thirteen-year-old who had his whole life in front of him and who one day took his life. My son was laughter and light. His tiny golden curls and huge smile as a baby won everyone over. As he grew more handsome his hair darkened and his eyes took on the clear green color of spring dew reflecting off the grass. He had a dry sense of humor, and even his teachers would smile and laugh when they were trying to be serious. He was a loving brother and helped his family when he could. He of course had his moments, but overall his heart was pure and good. He stood up to bullies for other kids and always had his brother's back. Being the size he was in eighth grade had its advantages.

Jason was not afraid of anything. He was the kind of person you can't help but be drawn to. I know as parents we like to believe all of our children will become or do something amazing with their lives, but Jason was the real Macoy, meant for greatness. That's what I wanted them to remember.

So closed casket it was, and the rest of the night went by like much of the last few days: inside the hot, red tornado trying to wish away what was now my reality.

Chapter 4: Accept

Memoir II

Accept: believe or come to recognize (an opinion, explation, etc.) as valid or correct.

June 30, 2011

Grief, husbands, and the joy of getting peed on!

I know, just like me to start with an absurd title, but if you know me, it fits all too well. I am grieving a terrible loss. Grieving is almost too mild a word. I am in constant pain and bleeding, if you will, from the heart on an hourly basis. So, to find relief I cling to those young ones around me. I live through their eyes, their joy, the simple way they live without pain. I have bonded very closely with my son's friends and, of course, my other three boys, for whom I live. This is what carries me through and makes the everyday livable.

So here I share the story of my beloved twins, for whom innocence still remains and the recognition of today's "polite" standards do not apply. Also keep in mind that these two beautiful boys are just four years old and a product of me and a father who finds humor in ANY bodily function.

After a very long day of continuous potty trips, wrestling, whining about toys, and their teenage brother on the XBOX all day, I found myself at the joyous moment of bath time. I say joyous because we all know that bedtime follows bath time! I follow my regular routine of filling the bath, undressing the boys, taking them to the potty, and setting them in the perfectly warm water.

As I sit looking at my angelic twins, I am suddenly hit in the face by a stream of urine that would rival any pressure washer found at Home Depot. As I scream at Petey to stop peeing on his mother, I find to his extreme delight that his aim has hit my mouth, and I am now screaming more. I turn around and immediately wash the foul fluid from my face and tongue only to be met by a second stream of hot liquid that my other twin has found a euphoric delight in delivering. Fortunately for me, though his brother's PSI is great, Joey's is unmatched.

Within seconds I am once again drenched in urine and tears are running with the yellow streams down my face. I pick up the closest phone to call my adoring husband and explain my situation. Expecting sympathy and kind words, I am met with whoops of laughter followed by a play-by-play to all the firefighters at the station. After a few moments, my loving husband promises a day of rest for me. How can I possibly expect him not to find that funny?

Yes, it's funny, and yes, I laugh. These are the small moments in life that make everything so special, so real, so precious. Quickly rinsing off, I found myself holding my children in my arms and falling asleep with them instead of watching my own shows or calling my friends.

It's these moments that can pull you through, these moments where your friends and family and even work mean nothing; the children bring the solace.

This is dedicated to all my son's friends, all of you who have reached out to me and made my suffering easier by including me in your life.

I Love You. JASON FOREVER, FOREVER JASON.

* * *

TODAY

My perception of life had been completely turned upside down. Everything that seemed to matter so much before losing Jason now did not even get a thought. I CLEARLY saw what I had only scratched the surface on before my Jason was lost.

In *Good Will Hunting*, Robin Williams's character Sean said, "You don't know about real loss, 'cause it only occurs when you've loved something more than yourself."

As a parent, you experience this for the first time in its truest form. That human, tiny little human you created looking at you like he does Superman. You are his whole world, and he is the only thing that brought color to yours. The reason it all makes sense, the reason we fight through another day, the reason we will drive on fumes just to create a legacy for them, our children through blood or otherwise. The ones whom we call family. We are their protectors, and they give us true purpose.

When I lost one, it was like all his bright color, his light, his greatness dispersed into the world and lit up everything that was good, everything that truly mattered. Things I, without question, loved more than myself.

When you can tap into that state of mind it all becomes so simple, and you have no time to sweat the small things. Each second ticks by and is gone way too fast to waste outside the space of kindness. That's where I found my first step back to the living, back into the color that had been taken from me: through Jason's friends and a mutual purpose.

Jason had touched so many people in the numerous schools he had attended, as we had to move around a bit in the market bubble burst. His baseball crews, friends he had been inseparable with since age four. We all came together and decided to start a charity to gather gently used equipment and raise funds so inner city Little Leagues could continue to thrive for low-income families: Jason's Propulsion League.

Jason's birthday following his death had been on Mother's Day, May 8, 2011. It was on this day three sets of parents, their kids, and friends held our first board meeting, and I posted my first online video of Jason.

Even back then, I always felt an overwhelming desire to tell the world about him, about my Jason and his story. That desire only grew as the years went by.

We began our heavy planning, and before I knew it, we were into the summer, and I was spending every day with my children and Jason's friends and parents. That's how we all made it through the first gruesome months: together.

Brian and Jason had both gone to the same school with a set of triplets since the age of four. Two of them had played baseball with Jason every year, and they spoke every day. Brian was in the same grade, so all five of them stayed close. After losing Jason, Brian just wanted to be with them. He had never been alone, never. Like a twin, he had lost a deep part of his soul when Jason died. He suffered his own kind of phantom pain on top of dealing with his personal demons. Yet, he did it. He needed to be with his friends, but when I would look at him, I could see the steel in his face, the resolve to push down those demons.

In these moments I would think back to that day. The day he held my hand, willing me to hold it together. Jason threw him his mojo that day. Almost like he couldn't entirely leave his brother alone without him. Before the twins, before Pete, it was just us, and now a third of that was gone forever. He needed his friends as much as I needed him and the twins.

During that time I also felt the deep sting of reality as word spread and stories became "tall tales" and twisted as they passed through each ear in whispers. The word suicide slides around in the shadows until you finally let it bite you, and as bad as the bite is, the venom that spreads after is worse. I will never forget one mother approaching me at a football game I was at for one of Jason's friends.

"I hope your son embraced Jesus. He will be damned for taking his own life." Out of the blue she had come up beside me and spewed out what I perceived to be filth from her mouth. How dare anyone say that about my son?

"He was baptized, yes, but even if he wasn't it was an accident. Even if it wasn't an accident, my son was more worthy of Heaven than either you or me. My boy never even got to kiss a girl let alone learn what a true sin is."

I turned briskly and put my head down, walking away. There it was, the thing I was still trying to protect him from: the way people now looked at us, the change in the way they remembered Jason and treated us. Some friends just stopped talking to us altogether. I suppose that's with any loss of a child, but some now wouldn't let their kids come over. Some felt it odd I spent all my time with my children and Jason's friends. One even told her daughter flat out, "A boy of thirteen doesn't just blow his brains out, there is something wrong with that family."

And they would not come over. I began to come to terms that I couldn't hide from it any longer, and as I accepted the fate of forever being labelled, I wept for my son. How was I to build his legacy on a foundation of suicide? That's how the first 100 days went. That's when acceptance of the word suicide started to set in, and the stigma became my enemy.

Chapter 5: Suffer

Memoir III

Suffer: experience or be subjected to
(something bad or unpleasant)

August 19, 2011

The needs of the many outweigh the needs of the few.

I read a post on Facebook that my son wrote today. A post speaking of his recently departed brother. A brother with whom he shared a room for eleven years and a life for thirteen. The same grade, same friends, a shared life. In his post, he stated how much he missed Jason, how he felt "half" of himself was gone and how being without him as he entered high school felt.

All I could think was "This is my fault, this is my responsibility. After all, I am his mother, the one who looks out for him, the one who failed his brother."

I cannot take his pain, something I would do without hesitation. I cannot bring his brother back, something I would suffer ANYTHING to accomplish. Each day he wakes to only one going to high school, only one eating breakfast, only one taking the bus. He sees himself completely alone.

It is these moments that intensifies the pain of losing a child. Intensified because that pain is also carried on the shoulders of siblings. So buried in our suffering we forget they too are treading water. Jason was his brother, his best friend, his comfort, his guardian. I cannot take his pain, I cannot make him feel better. I can only be here for him, be here to listen, to feel what he feels and to show him it can be done.

Living that is. You can live in suffering.

Every day I would rather be burned and beaten, cut and tortured, than realize my son is dead. Yet, I have other children. Children who are also in great pain. Children who need me, depend on me, and look to me for guidance and how to move on. For this, I say in my own Trekkie way:

"The needs of the many outweigh the needs of the few" says Spock.

"Or the one," adds Captain Kirk,

Sounds ridiculous, but it resonates with me, and in this I stay strong—as strong as I can—for him, my son who has lost his brother, lost his other half.

Dedicated to my sweet Brian. For you I will stay, for you I go on.

JASON FOREVER, FOREVER JASON

* * *

TODAY

I had forgotten to look at my other children's pain. I knew it was there, of course, but I was not LOOKING at it. I had pushed it aside, in that deep hidden cupboard we stuff things we cannot handle. In doing so I began to isolate myself, and that's where you can feel alone, and only darkness follows that path.

I had been searching social media, always looking for clues or answers to the why, when I stumbled upon Brian's post. That was a wake-up call. That was a warning sign. Time to pull my head out of my own labyrinth of bullshit and talk to my kid. The arrogance in thinking I was the only one suffering quickly dispersed when I saw that pain reflected in Brian's eyes. How dare I step away from that responsibility, and how dare I assume I am the only one who cannot handle it.

The next several posts show my resolve and commitment to make a stand of some type. I had no idea what exactly; it was like having that word stuck on the tip of your tongue yet you cannot remember it.

I felt a deep pull. I had a shadow of what needed to be done, but I could not see it.

Not yet.

But, I started to feel the need to speak out and tell my story. It seemed my eyes had been opened to a great many things since losing my boy—one of them how many suicides there were and the ripple effect.

The statistics were mind boggling, and the stigma made it almost impossible to just say the word without immediate assumptions and judgement. Even I had a mindset this was an ugly, shameful secret, and you should just be quiet. I was deeply conflicted. My Jason was not ill, disturbed, or vile in any way, yet he had taken his life, and the word for that act immediately carries that image.

Jason had been baptized, we lived in faith. My son was a wonderful soul, good to people, loyal to friends, and forever reliable. Yes, he obviously was suffering somewhere inside, but on the outside, he was a joyous child. Suicide did not suddenly make him evil and not worthy of Heaven or whatever higher plane we are destined for. Like I told the closed-minded mother from the football game: he never even had his first kiss. Try and tell me his fate is worse than that of a serial killer.

That woman's comment was wrong, so far off base I became angry. Angry enough to override my grief in that moment. I was going to fight this stigma because I was proud of my son then, now, and forever.

Jason Forever, Forever Jason

Chapter 6: Suicide

Memoir IV

Suicide: the act or an instance of taking one's own life voluntarily and intentionally.

September 13, 2011

Making a difference with the word suicide.

Many don't understand why we would expose ourselves with such a tragedy or why we wanted to "hurt" other family members with such a move.

What they don't understand is it isn't about them, it's about my son and how we can help others find a way to understand and cope with the loss of a child. Does it matter how he passed, or is it the fact that his family and friends have found a way to honor him and keep it together? Cancer, car accident, murder, suicide . . . losing a child in any manner is unbearable. Many believe we have done something good for the families and friends grieving after such a loss. It is a courageous thing to open yourself up to ridicule and speculation, but it's even more courageous to make it through each and every day after such a loss.

Before you make judgment, think of what the family has already endured. Before you throw that stone, open your eyes to the broken bones of their lives. Whatever accusation you may have with regard to "fault," they are feeling guilt with each breath they take knowing their child is dead. Whatever punishment you wish to inflict with cruel words and assumptions of the family and their dynamic, it's nothing compared to the daily kick in the stomach we feel when we think of our child. We live in a continuous nightmare that leaves us drowning in agony and sorrow without end. What we need is support, understanding, and kindness. The old saying "It takes a village to raise a child" does not stop if the child passes. The village is still needed by the family, just in a different way. In a way of support and understanding.

Jason was an extremely bright and exuberant young man. He had a God-given talent in sports, an easy way about him, and a humor that even made his teachers laugh when he should have been in trouble. Like any other teen, he had his moments too. He was a typical teenager with faults, just as we are typical parents with faults. There isn't one moment I am ashamed of my child nor one moment I will not openly talk about him. I am proud of my son, proud of his family, proud of his friends. Join our movement to bring these families awareness of our compassion and empathy. Help them to realize there is nothing to be ashamed of. Open your heart to the possibility of uplifting them instead of bringing them down.

Join our village.

JASON FOREVER, FOREVER JASON

* * *

TODAY

I had accepted it was intentional, or at least let it live in my thoughts he did go upstairs and put the gun in his hands. I still told myself it was an accident, that he just meant to hold it in his hands, that he wanted us to find him sitting there and ask him why.

In my mind, I truly believed he just wanted a way to tell us what he was thinking without saying it, to take him seriously if we saw he was holding a gun and he meant to inflict harm upon himself.

Maybe that was it, but regardless of his thoughts in those few moments, he pulled the trigger.

That's how painful it is when your child takes their own life. You keep finding ways to say it's not true. I quickly learned as I allowed that possibility of this intention to sink in, that the judgement, blame, and accusation grew and attached itself to us. We had friends who stopped calling and just avoided us at gatherings. Brian's friends' parents could be thinking they did not want their kid to go to a house someone passed in.

The truth was they did not want their children around "that" family.

Rumors spread in the schools, nasty things like Jason's own brother Brian had shot him and we were trying to cover it up, claiming suicide. Other accusations, like we, his parents, had been abusive, strict, and he took his life to get away from us. Then there were the trolls online who had crept on his social media and posted pictures of my son with a target for his head and a gun in his hands, taking the time to actually edit something like that so they could cause direct pain to his family and friends. I had to shut the page down. It was a hideous act and we had been targeted because apparently they find fun in pain.

From that time at the football game where I had my first taste of the stigma to just a few short months later, I had realized it was not going away and had the potential to destroy us as a family. The monster society has created with the word suicide was a huge part of the problem. Combine the two, my sorrow and those parents and friends who fell away, let alone trying to maintain some semblance of normality for the kids, I was losing my tenuous foothold on sanity because of one thing, one word: suicide.

If the word was cancer, would it be the same? If the word was murder, plane crash, diabetes, anything other, would we be treated as such? Would my son have been trolled and strung up as a sinner?

If it had been anything other than this shunned and terrifying act, parents would personally come over, bring food, lend a shoulder to cry on. Friends and students would gather and mourn openly, support my other boy and rally around him. Yet it was and is suicide, and that stigma ignites sheer hatred, terror, suspicion, doubt, and accusation. Suicide is a monster, a virus. So much so, it's treated as if it is infectious and the family who are afflicted are the carriers of the disease.

I had started to research, both in statistics and causes. I felt the need to understand what the fuck had happened and how the hell it happened to us. How did my kid just wake up and be dead before 8:30

on a random Tuesday morning? I was so angry, I would stand in the shower and just scream and sob. Everything in my life seemed to be swirling into chaos, and I was in a frenzy to find answers.

This is how I had approached everything that had challenged me in my life. I did not like NOT having the answers. I am excellent at research, and I crave solution. I consider myself to be a solutionist, and my tenacity and determination to solve the puzzle and win is built into my genes. Yet, this was a puzzle I could not solve. Ever. I would never have the answer, and I was livid, crazy drunk on the need to figure it out, when really, the "it" was something I could not even identify yet.

I was determined to show people, to tell people, to do something. How is it that this horrific, life-altering moment could keep getting worse? How much more could I take, and what was I going to do to keep myself from stepping back into complete insanity, from turning my guts inside out? I needed to share my story, and that's what I started to do, what I was driven to do. The following article by *The Arizona Republic* was the beginning of me sharing my story.[1]

Recent Arizona teen suicides put eye on prevention

Recent Arizona deaths reveal need to teach coping skills

by **Laurie Merrill and Kerry Fehr-Snyder** - Sept. 6, 2011 12:00 AM *The Arizona Republic*

---

1 Merrill, Laurie, and Kerry Fehr-snyder. "Speaking out on Teen Suicide." PressReader.com. *The Arizona Republic, September 6, 2011.* https://www.pressreader.com/usa/the-arizona-republic/20110906/282832187826479.

A Chandler teenager used a belt to hang herself in a closet in July.

In August, a Kyrene School District student was found swinging in a noose at school.

Last March, a week to the day after a Scottsdale boy killed himself, a thirteen-year-old used his father's loaded gun to take his life.

In Chandler and Scottsdale alone, six teens ages thirteen to sixteen have taken their own lives since March.

They hanged themselves or shot themselves. Some were bullied, one was on antidepressants, two had access to loaded guns. At least one played violent video games.

The deaths have reverberated around the Valley. Thousands are grieving the children who were too young to die. Many have left condolences on Facebook pages.

Two girls from Chandler's Basha High School started the No Bear Left Behind group to create awareness about suicide after two students, a former student, and a parent killed themselves this year.

The others attended Aprende Middle School in Chandler, Explorer Middle School in Phoenix, and Cheyenne Traditional School and Desert Mountain High School in Scottsdale.

The cases reflect Arizona's high teen-suicide rate, tenth in the nation, and the need for programs that teach teens coping skills and teach parents and friends the warning signs of suicide.

Experts say the teen-suicide rate has dipped, but it is still an epidemic.

Last year, 53 Arizona youths killed themselves, and more than 10,000 made attempts. Bullying victims are two to nine times more likely to consider suicide. More than one in three children have been threatened online.

The suicide rate among all ages is double the homicide rate, and a leading cause of death in Arizona, according to the Arizona Suicide Prevention Coalition. Unrestrictive gun laws are also a factor, as it is in other states with high rates, experts say.

Underlying factors

Sexual orientation, family arguments, bullying, relationship issues, and depression are some factors that can contribute to teen suicide.

But experts say there is no single answer. The one common denominator is pain—pain so overwhelming it dims reasoning, pain so excruciating it feels like it will never end.

Recent Arizona teen suicides put eye on prevention

"They were in such unbearable pain within themselves they couldn't see any other way out," said Nikki Kontz, Teen Lifeline clinical director and board president of the Arizona Suicide Prevention Coalition.

"But there is hope out there. It is about reaching out and trying to get it."

Mothers' suggestions

In interviews, two of the teens' mothers had suggestions for preventing future deaths. They said don't keep loaded guns in the house, think carefully before putting your child on antidepressants, and limit their time playing violent video games, which may desensitize them to guns.

Most importantly, talk to your children and help them learn coping skills.

"Kids don't realize the finality," said Kimberly Tocco, the mother of a thirteen-year-old baseball player who fatally shot himself. "They don't realize that by ending the pain, they are ending THEM."

Tocco, of Scottsdale, is open and public about the death of her son, Jason Legere. *The Arizona Republic* does not report on suicides in most cases.

Tocco wants to use her experience to help others. She writes a blog, I Lost My Child, I Lost Myself, and is writing a book, "Jason Forever, Forever Jason."

She has started a non-profit foundation, Jason's Propulsion League, to raise money for underprivileged baseball players.

Tocco said Jason's death was accidental. She believes he grabbed her gun from under her mattress, which he did not know was loaded, to get her attention after an argument. It went off, striking his head.

Police said it was intentional.

Agonizing guilt

Tocco and her husband, Peter Tocco, who have three other sons, blame themselves.

"The most unnatural thing in the world is for a parent to lose a child," said Peter, a Scottsdale firefighter.

Kimberly wears Jason's clothes, his jewelry. She has a tattoo in his honor. Pain racks her when she thinks he will never kiss a girl, never go to high school. "I feel 100 percent guilty," she said.

She describes her agony in her book.

"This was not a wound, this is a ripping of my very soul, a destruction of my being. This you do not recover from, you do not forget, and you do not feel the ease of acceptance with time."

Effect of bullying

Two other recent teens who killed themselves were bullied in school, but their loved ones say it was not part of their deaths.

"He never let anyone who bullied him get him down," one family member wrote on Facebook. "He was looking forward to this school year so much, and he loved all of his classes, teachers, and classmates."

Some bullies continued their cruelty after the teens died. At least one page has been the victim of "trolling," the posting of inconsiderate or mean messages.

For Tocco, the best medicine is to talk about her son, but it is often awkward. "If I bring it up, they don't talk. People need to give friends the opportunity to talk about their child."

* * *

TODAY

Somehow, though extremely painful, it felt "right" to speak openly about it. It sparked the embers of purpose lying in wait. I was yearning for purpose and meaning, the ever-present and pounding urgency of why this happened. I was going mad trying to figure it out, with the constant questions and anger at God, the universe, everyone and everything. This I could not fix or even begin to figure out.

He was gone, and there was no bringing him back. I was spiraling, sinking back into the red tornado to get away to stop the pain.

I just wanted him back, but there was also this thing sitting at the base of my throat, hidden deep in my broken heart. An entity, really. I just wanted to tell everyone everything I was feeling. I thought somehow it would make a difference or it would give his death meaning. I did not know other than I wanted to talk about it, share my son and who he was, that he was not just this kid who took his life. It was not just a want, it was a NEED.

But no one was listening, and why would they? I was just a mom grieving her son who had committed suicide, shot himself in the head. I would often hear or think I heard them whispering.

"Poor girl, there must be some heavy shit at that house. Just let her ramble on and get it out. It's like therapy for her, her blog is so sweet."

It was falling on deaf ears, and really, I didn't even know what I was trying to say, but I recognized the stigma, the pity they had for me. All of them. I appreciated and despised it at the same time. I was never the receiver of pity. I was always the spitfire, the one who could do anything, the one who would never give up. I conquered. As Naomi Judd once stated, "You can only be the victim once, after that you are a volunteer."

I did not want to be a victim, a survivor of suicide. Yet they were right, because here I was, a small lump of dust in the corner. This had beat me down, crushed and ground me into nothing. I was fighting but it could not be seen on the outside. At times I would look in the mirror and a woman I did not even begin to recognize would be looking back at me.

I remembered the times I had to look in the mirror every day after leaving my abusive first husband. Every day I was supposed to look in the mirror and tell that girl who was looking back I loved her. It was a very difficult thing to do at the time, so much so I used sticky notes that said "I love you" stuck to the mirror to remind myself. It worked, though, and over time I began to see things that had been hidden away. Comparing the two, this woman looking back at me was a hopeless cause compared to the one who had rebuilt her life after abuse. This woman I looked at now was dead inside, and whatever it was I was feeling fell to the wayside as the waves of pain and grief took over once again.

Chapter 7: Fate

Memoir V

Fate: the reason for which something is done or created or for which something exists

October 11, 2011

Strange, but true.

"It's happened again. I had that dream again," a shaken woman speaks into her phone urgently.

"What dream, what has happened? Honey, calm down, this is just a dream, only a dream, right?" her husband on the other end of the phone assures her.

"I don't know, it's the same dream. We were hiking again, all of us. Once again I heard the scream and I look over to see him slipping over the edge. I run and never reach him, all I see is him falling from the edge, hear his scream, then sudden silence as he hit the bottom. I can't understand, this is really scaring me! I

have never dreamt of anyone dying, let alone my child. It was so raw, and I couldn't save him. He just falls to his death each time and I am left feeling like it was just so real."

"Look, it's just a dream, we all have strange dreams. Was it the same child?" her husband hesitantly asks.

"That's the thing, it was the same boy, the same situation, the same 'real' feeling. I couldn't reach him in time."

Hearing the panic in her voice, her husband calmly assures her, "OK, OK, let's just talk about this. Sometimes people can have the same dream again and again and it's still just that, a dream."

The woman takes a deep breath, realizes he is right, she is being silly, and tells herself. Besides, it's been months since the last dream like this. Yet, the lingering feeling of foreboding is stronger than the last.

The family continues on their everyday life, typical of any household with hardworking parents and four children. Several months go by and she does not have the dream again. Her children are doing well and her life is good. Then one morning it happens, her son, the same one from the dream, dies. She struggles to reach him and save his life, but no matter what she does, he passes from this world, and she is left with the reality of his true death. Not a dream, not a nightmare, but a living horror of a mother unable to save her son's life.

In the many hours she spends pondering the coincidence of the dreams and her now real life, she can't help but think it may have been mother's intuition, a warning of what was to come. She also puts something else together that makes the hairs on the back of her neck stand.

His birthday is May 8, 1997. 5+8= ***13****, her son's age when he died. 5+8+1+9+9+7=* ***39****, the age of his mother when he died. His birthday predicted the ages we would both be at his death.*

His favorite number is thirteen, and one he always tried to get for his baseball jersey. If he did not get thirteen, he would always get eleven.

The date of his death, March 22, 2011. 3+2+2+2+1+1= 11, the other jersey number.

His mother's birthday, March 11, 1972. 3+1+1+1+9+7+2= 24, the age she was when she carried him. My birthday predicted the age I would be when I conceived him.

He was born on a Mother's Day weekend, and his birthday following his death was ON Mother's Day.

Yes, strange.

And yes, all true.

* * *

TODAY

It's the guilt that whispers in your ear late at night, when you are afraid to close your eyes because all you see is his dead body. Guilt that greets you first when you open your eyes after what little sleep you do get. Guilt is greedy and enjoys sucking the life out of you. I would think about all the little things I could have, should have done. Even down to listening to my dreams.

You look for the signs you missed, because after all, there HAD to be a reason, had to have been something that alluded to him being stressed or depressed. I looked at everything I had gone through while he was just a baby, everything as he grew older, anything that would have contributed to his doing this. Was it my fault? I always came to the same answer: yes, it was my fault.

People would say differently, and for years I struggled with it, and still do. Yet, here is the cold, hard truth: I am his mother, it is my job to protect him, nurture him, bring him into adulthood safe and with the best I could give him. In all of these I failed, and I was beating myself up for it over and over again.

How did I think this could never happen to me? How did I assume he was happy just because he never complained? How did I not see he was feeling all of the stress for the short sale of our home, the diagnosis and care of both his oldest brother with bipolar disorder and his youngest with autism? How did I not see the pressures he had holding all of this on his shoulders and not complaining? Not saying a word because he did not want to add to the pile of shit we had to deal with. Not saying anything because he knew we would probably blow it off as teenage problems in the face of the "real" problems of the world.

It was my fault, and it is MY guilt, and slowly I came to terms with it, but it still lingers, still whispers. Yet, I started to hear other whispers too, ones that shock me back to reality and my purpose. But not before I almost gave up on all of it and gave into the pain and sorrow.

I heard it, very distinctly, that voice again in my head.

"Mom, Mom, what are you doing?"

It just was not rational, hearing his voice inside my head, and not for the first time. Sitting in his bed after the first move and just before the first interview with Connie Colla, a news channel reporter, I HEARD IT. I HEARD HIM.

"Mom, MOM! What are you doing? Enough of the pity party, it's time."

I did listen that time, though I figured it was just my mind playing tricks, and it was comforting to imagine it was Jason, by my side, urging me to do something, anything but cry. Now, as we got closer to the two-year mark entering into 2013, I heard it again.

"Mom, Mom, what are you doing? I am not there to live the life I was meant to have. To be the superstar you knew I COULD be. So you need to do it for me. Enough with the pity party, it's time."

It was Jason. I know that now, without hesitation or doubt. Too much of what I am about to tell you is more than coincidence. It was and is . . . FATE.

In many ways, a parent that loses a child will never be able to completely accept they are no longer physically with us. So instead, we look for signs, a spark of evidence they are somewhere, be it energy, spirit, another dimension. We cannot fully let go. Our souls are bound to them by the extreme and unconditional love for that child, all of our children. Just like the shadow pain of a lost limb, we still feel them. I had a very difficult time with this. I did not care if there was another place or world our loved ones went to. I wanted him here, NOW. I was red with anger, black with despair and grief, and I was falling into that dark red tunnel again. The quiet place I go in the eye of the tornado.

I was drinking every day. Not a lot, but enough to be drunk by 10 p.m. I was not eating, not caring about where my future was going, and I was contemplating suicide myself. Just a few weeks before, I sat outside in the dark alone, knife in my hand, ready to slit my throat and dive to the bottom of the pool. I felt the tiny little breakthroughs of something called life when I played with the twins or helped inner city kids with baseball, but it was not enough. The pain was winning, the deep fog and dark red tornado were closing in again, and for good this time. I remember very clearly: the night was chilly, the sky very clear, and I was crouched down, serrated knife in my hand . . . Do it quick and jump in. Quick. Now!

I couldn't do it. In the same instant I urged myself on, visions of the twins mourning their mother, and Brian, oh, GOD, my Brian. He would not survive another loss, especially the loss of his mom. So I looked up at the sky and let the water flow from my eyes and began to scream. A savage, guttural scream full of pain, and it felt good to release that. Good enough to stay my hand and give it one more day. I let myself simmer from the boil that had erupted and dragged my body inside, grateful and almost relieved in its raw moment of clarity.

In that moment, I realized I could carry this pain and push through. In that tiny flicker of time, I realized living with pain is possible as long as you find a way to bring joy. My joy has always been my children and giving my family abundance. It was time, yet how do I do that from the battered, broken pieces I had become?

Yet I get ahead of myself. Let's go back to the first year and the first Thanksgiving dinner.

Chapter 8: Traditions

Memoir VI

Traditions: the transmission of customs or beliefs from generation to generation.

November 18, 2011

Thanksgiving dinner, a new tradition.

Jason loved turkey, potatoes, and gravy—especially because he had to have Thanksgiving dinner twice on turkey day. He would have it with us as a family, then he and his brother would go to his grandparents' house and have it again. No matter how hard I tried to cook the perfect feast or even order the perfect meal, he would always say, "No one beats Nana's Thanksgiving dinner!"

This year I don't have my Jason taunting me about my cooking. This year we will have one less plate at the table. This year I am not grateful.

For Jason, I have done many things to keep his memory and spirit alive. I wear his shirts, sing his songs, talk to his friends, use his inspiration to build on his charity: Jason's Propulsion League. But some things I will not, no, cannot do, because he is not here to do them with.

One of those things is enjoying the warmth and inviting meal we as Americans have made an annual tradition. I cannot sit and enjoy the food my son will never get to have again. To think he only had thirteen times to actually partake in the holiday is sickening. To think I am still here after thirty-nine of them is so completely unfair.

So, I will not be eating the beautifully cooked turkey, the creamy mashed potatoes, or the aromatic gravy. Instead, I will watch as the rest of my family and friends fill up on the traditional delights. Just watch, as my son will be doing on that day from his Heavenly place.

It will be a new tradition for me, and one I will keep until I can hold his hand in Heaven, and we can do it together.

JASON FOREVER, FOREVER JASON

* * *

TODAY

I still recall that day, feeling like I was swimming through Jell-O. Everything was difficult, even the lifting of my arms, picking up the fork, putting the food in my mouth. I gagged it down, felt it stick in the back of my throat, just eating for it to go down.

Drink more wine

I had been going to his best friends' house almost daily with my oldest son Brian. They were triplets, and they had two younger siblings, so going over there for me was like flying off to Neverland. At any given moment I was surrounded by eight children that had all known and loved my Jason. For that Thanksgiving the family invited us over to spend it with them, as we had practically moved in. It was not easy on them, there were many whispers that floated through the schools and our once mutual friends.

"Why is she always around children? It's weird? Are you afraid to leave her there alone at your house with your kids? Her son blew his brains out after all."

After a while I could not subject the family to that kind of gossip and rumor. It was not fair to the kids nor to the parents who just wanted to show us comfort. They were being labelled by the stigma. Once again, I saw the face of cruelty in the way society treated suicide. If I had lost him to cancer, would they still spread these rumors?

No they would not.

Chapter 9: Holidays

Memoir VII

Holiday: a day of festivity or recreation
when no work is done

December 24, 2011

The Night before Christmas

'Twas the night before Christmas and I still hadn't decorated the tree

I just couldn't hang those ornaments we once bought as a family of three

We had a tradition, Brian, Jason, and I

A new ornament every year as Christmas came by

Even as our family grew with a new dad and two new brothers

Our tradition went on, a new ornament each year, exactly as we started

Yet, now having pulled the lid off the first box

I am greeted with the memories that for one, they will stop

I look at his stocking and the ornaments he picked out

And my tears start to fall and my anguish turns to a terrible shout

"I can't do this, I can't do this! Not without him here!"

And the lid goes back on, my sanity I fear

I retreat to my room, but not before a sweet voice meets my ears

"Daddy, Daddy, let's decorate for Mommy this year"

After a while, I return to the tree

Holding my breath, not sure I want to see

Decorate they had, yet with only the lights

So I am not bluntly reminded my son is not here on this night

I look at the twins and the oldest of my sons

And find I am thankful for all they have done

With a wipe of my tears and a reach for his old book

I carry on one tradition he would not overlook

I sit with the twins while the others listen to the lines

And I begin with the story, the one I read to him but thirteen times:

"'Twas the night before Christmas and all through the house . . ."

* * *

Today

You are never prepared for the "firsts." The first birthday, celebration, holiday, traditions: they hit you like whiplash. They pick you up and shake you over and over again, crushing and inflicting shock. You keep setting the table for them at meal times, you keep buying them gifts, baking their cakes, singing happy birthday. It's not something you can stop, and I had a hard time wrapping my head around it—yet I had to.

The wake-up call months ago kept me centered enough to realize my kids still needed their mother, but the holidays were another level altogether. A one-two punch, but that is part of the deal, the complete package when you have lost a child. You cannot change anything about that cold hard fact: they are no longer with us. It's an excruciating déjà vu you have to wrap your head around. Somehow, I had to pull my head out of the black abyss that always calls when I feel the pain of that day, the day he stopped breathing. I had to focus on those who needed me, and when I did a funny thing happened: I found my face tilted in a smile again as I read to the twins. I found I could feel something beyond the crushing despair when I saw my oldest laughing with his friends and building bonds to bridge the gap of his brother no longer with him every minute of every day. Just that was enough for me to say, "Just do it, get up and shake it off, you are here and you owe him that much."

I have been saying that to myself ever since that day. I owe him that much. To at the very least live. Not just survive, but truly LIVE.

Chapter 10: Propulsion

Memoir VIII

Propulsion: the action of driving or pushing forward

March 11, 2012

Opening Day ceremonies and the LIGHT behind Jason's Propulsion League.

Today, South Scottsdale Little League will be holding the Opening Day ceremonies of the 2012 Spring Season. Today, over eighteen children will get to play baseball because of Jason's Propulsion League. Today, the entire league has enough equipment, both new and used, to supply every child with what they need to play the game. Today is my birthday, and this is Jason's present to me.

When I lost my beloved son almost a year ago, I knew within days I could not let his spirit go even though I had to let his body go. I had to do something worthy of his beautiful compassion and his drive for greatness. He loved the game of baseball and he loved to make people laugh. He was always the one to give a kid the shirt off his back or cheer them up when they were down.

I remember a time when Jason was little and I was a single mom with not much to spare. He wanted to play in an afterschool basketball program, but I just couldn't afford it. When his friend's mom heard this, she generously offered to cover the fee, and Jason was able to play. The solution suddenly became clear: a charity that helps underprivileged children play baseball by paying the fees and providing equipment.

It took a while to organize the business plan, and Jason's grandmother came up with the name. I took a large portion of the money donated for Jason's funeral expenses and started the long process of paying the fees and filing the paperwork to become a fully registered nonprofit corporation. My very close friends offered to be part of the company, and together we raised enough funds to see this glorious day with South Scottsdale Little League become a reality.

So, on this day I offer a piece of my son and what I know his charity brings to those children who otherwise could not play. In his own words and the light behind Jason's Propulsion League. . .

BASEBALL

One of the most amazing games I have ever played was last year on my White Sox team. In the last inning, the score was tied up, one to one. I had pitched a pretty good game. I was up to bat, bases loaded with two outs. I had two strikes, last pitch right down the middle. I swung, I felt the connection of the ball and the bat, the ball flew out. I had hit my first home run of the game as the ball flew over the fence. We beat the them five to one. That was the most amazing game I have ever had.

~ Jason Paul Legere

This is what JPL gives to the children we sponsor. This is how Jason leaves his mark in our world. The spirit of pure joy only a child can have and the opportunity to give it to them.

Thank you, my son.

JASON FOREVER, FOREVER JASON

* * *

TODAY

There had been signs Jason was still with me. Call it what you will, but I call it a nod from him letting me know he was proud of me, telling me to keep going. The first sign was the Tootsie Roll. Jason loved them, and I would find wrappers everywhere.

For the reception after his funeral, we had bowls of Tootsie Rolls on each table. It was here I reconnected with my sister's ex-husband. She had passed ten years earlier in the middle of a messy divorce. I had seen very little of her children, and this brought us back together. My sister's children were within a year of Jason's age, and I had missed them dearly. They had invited me back over to her house a few days later. It was strange going there again after so many years and seeing everything was pretty much the same as she had left it. All of her decorations and furnishings, it felt like she and Jason both wanted me to be there. I was able to catch up with her two children, which brought me some comfort as they are both so much like her.

During the visit I went to the kitchen and took a glass out of the cabinet and walked over to the refrigerator and pushed the glass under the ice dispenser. As the ice started to flow out, an empty Tootsie Roll wrapper fell out, randomly mixed in with the ice somehow. I stopped the ice immediately and stared. Even if somehow my sister's children had taken a Tootsie Roll from the funeral, how would they possibly time it to be placed in the ice dispenser just at the random time I decided I was thirsty, in a place I had not been to in ten years. That was Jason letting me know he was there and he was with me, pointing out something good that had happened after I lost him, that he was behind me, with me, and happy his mother was there.

There were many small things I would notice, but then again, you teeter on the edge of what is real and what you WANT to be real. This day, the Opening Day ceremonies of our first season in our efforts to help children, landed on my birthday. That in itself was a small light on a day I did not want to celebrate. That I should keep celebrating my birthday when he will never have another was difficult. Needless to say, not something I wanted to do, and this felt like a gift from him. I was wrong, the gift was still coming.

The real gift came when I was rummaging through his school papers. We had to move again, three houses in less than a year due to foreclosure and us having to rent. I was digging in boxes and came across that letter—the one I referenced to in the memoir. It looked to be an assignment on describing a great day in his life. It was proof to me he was proud of what I was doing, that his energy, light, spirit, whatever it may be, was right next to me.

Better yet, he was forever in my heart and I needed to listen. I needed to get out of my head and do what felt right and good, because that was key to pushing through another day. That was a light bulb—a tiny, dim Christmas-sized one, but it was there. The idea, no the realization, that by giving back I may find joy again . . . someday. I had that letter laminated and it sits with his baseball glove on my mantel to this day.

Chapter 11: Anger

Memoir IX

Anger: fill someone with anger, provoke anger in

April 28, 2012

I have four children, one just lives in Heaven.

It's so hard when people ask, "How many children do you have?" Do I say three because only three are alive? Do I say four because that's how many children I REALLY do have? If I say three, I don't have to explain what happened to my fourth child or why he is in Heaven. If I say three, I deny my child whom I gave birth to and raised for thirteen years. If I say four and one lives in Heaven, I am subjected to pity and stupid questions, like "Oh, I am so sorry, what happened?"

I realize people are not aware of horrific events that can occur in peoples' lives. I realize when someone says, "My child is in Heaven," it opens up a very uncomfortable moment that makes you feel like you need to respond. We don't need a response, we don't need a question, we just need you to nod your head and acknowledge our children. Offer condolences, heartfelt looks, but don't ask us what happened. You never know, and you never can predict the reaction. Some have lost their children to illness, some murder, and some suicide . . .

Don't ask, just acknowledge.

Let us speak of our children as we would if they were here. Let us be proud we raised and loved those children even though they may be living in the embrace of our Heavenly Father. Don't ask, "Did your child embrace Jesus? Did your child know God?"

REALLY? EXCUSE ME? My child was innocent, a boy who loved life, loved his family. Please show me a god who would not embrace him for the wonderful soul he is. Show me a religion that would deny the innocence of a child and an impulsive decision that brought him in the embrace of the Heavenly world.

I know this is a rant, but I speak for all the families, mothers, and friends who have lost loved ones under self-inflicted injuries. DO NOT ASK US, "So, what REALLY happened?" Are you kidding me? Do you really think that there is something different than what you have been told? Do you really think there is a juicy story behind the fact our children took their own lives? Have you seen CSI, Law & Order: Criminal Intent? Yes, there was an investigation, yes, there was extensive questioning, yes, there was an autopsy. It is what is. They made a choice, a terrible choice we as parents feel every minute of every day . . . deep and painful.

So stop judging, stop your sick thoughts of "What really went on in that house?" We love our babies, and we would do ANYTHING to get them back. We are not bad parents, we are not unstable or uncaring. We are families suffering more than you could ever imagine, and we need you to understand and let us talk about our children "Who live in Heaven."

* * *

Today

This was really hard for me to read and reflect on. We had just passed all the firsts, and when that day, the day he died came rolling around the first time, I could feel the anger looking for ways to lash out, even hurt. Compounding that was the stigma of suicide. It really felt as if we were walking around with a big dark cloud above our head that never went away. I well understood the concept of "life is not fair." Yep, had that down and understood. Yet, this was almost accusing in its simplicity and treated us as cursed, contagious even.

Oddly enough, people who did not give over to the traditional belief of what suicide is, they did not feel comfortable talking about it. One thing I needed to do was talk about Jason, and no one wanted to hear that outside our small circle who loved him deeply. It just was not done, and it began to alienate me from many people. I was so caught up in all the negativity, drinking, spiraling, questioning everything and everyone. It began to strip away at what little sanity I had left, and that was a place I knew I could not return from.

His birthday was coming up, another one he would miss, then I would have to face another Mother's Day, another Father's Day, another Fourth of July, Halloween. They were all coming back around, and I realized it would always be as such. Like a hamster wheel, over and over and over again, but there was no break. Like a really sick episode of *The Twilight Zone*, and I began to wonder when any of it was going to let up, stop the slow decay from the inside.

I wanted to spit in the faces of those who judged me, slap them and say, "How dare you!" I was not thinking of how to solve the gigantic issue, I just wanted it to go away and to be treated like a parent who has lost her child. That was something the stigma would never allow. How is it we could hear these tales of bravery after the loss of a loved one and cheer them on and support them, yet with that one word, suicide, you had to shut your mouth and not even bring it up. That one word swept it under the rug where society felt it belonged. Like the tiny light bulb, it was there, but my sorrow suffocated that thought and instead I just gave into the anger. I needed to let it run its course or I was going to give into the red, dark tornado, and that was a place I was not sure I would return from.

That is the "stages of grief," as they say. Though I can attest we go through them in different ways, each and every one of us. Like a fingerprint, we are all different, and the traditional process we read about in any book or article are far different when we actually go through it. Denial and isolation come first, then anger, bargaining, depression, and finally acceptance. I felt them all, or sometimes just one, and certainly not in this order. Yet they do show up in these stages and circulate, coming back, fading in and out, until you deal with them and find a way to work through them.

Chapter 12: Autopsy

Memoir X

Autopsy: a critical examination, evaluation, or assessment of someone or something past

August 7, 2012

When suicide is not suicide . . . or is it?

It has been a few months since my last post. Mainly, I have been undergoing much needed PTSD therapy. It was time for me to face the fact I cannot get through this without help—PROFESSIONAL help.

Two months ago, I received the medical examiner's report of my boy. Something I hesitated to send for since I wasn't completely sure what I would read it. As most of you know by now, we have always felt this was an accident and not suicide. However, with no one in the room and Jason having been so angry that morning, his death was ruled a suicide. As I read through the medical examiner's report, I was reminded of how perfect and happy my boy was.

"The body is that of a well-developed, well-nourished, white male adolescent whose appearance is compatible with the stated age of thirteen."

He goes on to describe the rest of his body with only two small scars on the knee and the incisions made for organ harvesting. HARVESTING: what a horrible word! Yet, I remind myself he has saved lives, given sight, and restored burned and wounded people with his donation.

After a bit we come to the Evidence of Injury page. As I read through, I am reminded of what I saw on that horrible day and how I wrapped his head in a towel so I could only see his nose and mouth, to give him CPR. Everything was as I expected until we came to this line . . .

"Evaluation of hands reveals a faint deposition of soot on the left hand between the thumb and the index finger."

Left hand . . . LEFT HAND. JASON IS RIGHT HANDED!

I began to scream and cry at the same time.

It was confirmation of his UNintentional act of suicide. Yet, it didn't really matter, didn't change anything. My child is still dead.

I called the medical examiner's office to request a reinvestigation. The report proved to me what I felt, what we ALL felt all along: Jason had no intention of ending his life. I tried to explain to them who Jason was, what happened that morning, etc. After a while they said they would look into it and call me back. I never received that call.

After four weeks I called back and asked to speak with the investigations department. It took them quite some time to explain to me why they would not change the manner of death on his certificate. It basically came down to no one in the room to testify otherwise, and the fact that he held the gun, he pulled the trigger. Suicide . . . Accidental or otherwise, Jason killed himself.

So all this has done is leave me in the same position, along with all those that know me and my family, heartbroken, lost, and terribly sad. I did, however, find one thing in all of this horror, one thing that sticks every day and pops up every time I hear someone judging another. There is a stigma that follows a child's family when he has taken his life, a stigma that is NOT fair, yet I have found acceptance. Just as Jason's heart was pure, as my heart is sure, and as our family's bond is unbreakable.

It is the heart that really matters in the end.

* * *

Today

I do not know why I sent for his autopsy report or why it is still in my side nightstand. Well, that is not true, it is there because it is the official last words to ever be written about my son by a medical examiner. Like we keep our children's shot records, report cards, medical files, this was the last I would ever have. I wanted that report, it belonged to my son, and in turn, to me. I thought maybe if I read it, I would better understand the why. I had requested the gun be destroyed, but this I wanted to keep with me.

I remember pulling over in the car, alone, and I began to read through it. I remember the water on my face and just curling over and screaming. My gut twisted as the simple words on the page spoke their poison. It was the worst thing I have ever read. The final entry in your child's baby book should not be his obituary and final autopsy. I was convinced Jason probably just wanted us to find him sitting on the side of the bed with a gun in his hands and not knowing what he was doing, accidentally pulling the hair trigger. When there was not a mention of his right hand having gun powder, I immediately thought, "Yes, that's proof, an accident." It was unintentional was what I WANTED to believe because you never really want to accept your child took their own life. You never want to face the fact that you could not protect your child . . . from himself. That you missed the most important job you will ever have and the only job that should be a priority: keeping your children safe, healthy, and alive. That is a jagged pill filled with shrapnel that will do more damage even after you swallow it.

It was not an accident, and in my efforts to prove it was not, I only did the opposite and swallowed that pill. I had called the ME's office a few times and left a message, and finally they called back and pointed out that when you turn a gun around on yourself, you hold it with two hands and the left gets most of the gun powder. He assured me he pulled the trigger in a deliberate fashion by the examination of the evidence. The depression that left its mark on my son's head stated that he held the gun solidly and did not flinch as he pulled the trigger. It sent me over the edge, and I finally gave into counseling after I almost cut into my artery with a small carpentry saw while drinking heavily. That was the shrapnel that came out of the jagged little pill.

I had resisted therapy and counseling, did not even want to go to groups. I felt like no one, not even the parents going through the same thing, understood how I felt. I couldn't keep dragging my friends down just wallowing. A person can only take so much of that before they fade away. When I finally realized I was looking for some way to take the label of suicide away, I had to question why. Why was it so damn important I prove it was anything other than what it was?

If I was preaching about the stigma and how suicide should be openly discussed, then I needed to be able to look in the mirror and say it to myself. My son killed himself, intentionally, to escape whatever pain or entrapment he was carrying on his mind. As his mother, that was my job to help him with that, and I failed. Part of me did not want the label because that was my own guilt staring back at me. It was time to stand up and figure out who the fuck I was and what I was going to do about it. Rob Thomas wrote a song called "Little Wonders." I was listening to it a lot because the twins were enthralled with the movie

Meet the Robinsons. That's how I came up with that last line in the memoir.

"It's the heart that really matters in the end." ~ Rob Thomas

Chapter 13: Path

Memoir XI

Path: the direction in which something is moving

October 28, 2012

It's been a while since I posted . . .

It's been a while since I updated everyone on how we are doing . . . BEEN A WHILE

Since I have heard his voice;

Since I have touched his warm skin;

Since I held him and laughed with him.

The last time I saw my beautiful baby, he was cold, he was stiff, he was dead.

The tube in his mouth because they couldn't remove it for "standard practice" reasons.

The bags on his hands so they could get accurate testing results.

My husband begging them to remove the bag so I could hold his hand.

My heart stopping as they promised to cover his forehead so I didn't see the bullet hole.

My beautiful boy, gone forever, his cold body all that is left.

Made the decision to donate his organs.

Made the decision to be strong for my children.

Made the decision to keep his memory alive.

Nothing has changed, every day the same, my beautiful boy is not here.

HOWEVER,

Nothing will stop me from honoring his memory;

Nothing will make me feel he is not worthy of greatness;

Nothing, NOTHING, will ever make me ashamed of my son, he did what he did, but he was and is the best of me!

www.jplleague.org

* * *

Today

One thing had become very clear when I started focusing on what I needed to do in order to make sense of what I was going through. I had to find something that motivated me to get up out of bed, beyond the duties and routine of caring for a family. A purpose just for myself that could grow as I nurtured it. Something that would fill the time I would have spent with Jason. Something worthy of him and that made me WANT to put effort into living. That would give me motivation to step out of my bubble of pity and at least "try."

The little charity I started did that for me. I would collect gently used equipment from the families and friends of all the teams he was with and played on over the years. Sometimes I would get a $400 bat that had been barely used, and giving that over to the league where an inner city kid had never even held a bat like that felt good. That was something Jason would do, so I kept at it, getting news channels involved when I would come across a field and equipment room in shambles. We gave thousands of dollars, raised through small get-togethers and gatherings where we spoke about Jason and the why behind the charity.

There was a very specific reason I chose to raise money and equipment for inner city kids. As a single mother when Brian and Jason were little, I could not afford to pay the registration fees one year. Jason had been playing baseball, and that year he asked if he could also try basketball. Being such a tall, athletic kid, naturally he was very good at it. But, that year I just did not have the extra funds.

One of Jason's friends had mentioned this to his mother, and she called me.

"Hi there, Kimberly, listen, my son has decided he does not want to play basketball this year, but the fee is nonrefundable. Since we already paid, do you think Jason would like his spot?" I was floored and humbly accepted.

I never forgot that, and now I wanted to do that for other children as well.

Pay the fees so kids could play, and gather equipment so leagues could loan gear out to the kids for the season. We even provided all the equipment for Miracle League at Victory Lane Sports Park, built for special needs children, the last fields my boy played on.

Giving was my antidepressant, my therapy, and my reason to put more effort into my "every day." It allowed me to openly speak of my son at the events and uplift the people there by giving them something to remember Jason by other than suicide. His name was now passed around as making a difference, changing lives, giving kids a chance. My path had been made clear: to serve is what my heart yearned for. To serve by giving.

Chapter 14: Why

Memoir XII

Why: for what cause reason or purpose

January 26, 2013

Aftermath

Coming up on almost two years, 677 days to be exact, I am reflecting on my world after losing my beautiful boy. Much of the aftermath is ever changing, yet ever the same.

Time has trickled by so very slowly, minutes seem endless when I look at his many pictures and wonder, "How is it he is not here?" Sometimes I can't even look at the walls where I have hung my favorites of him; seeing his reflection feels like a hot knife searing my gut. I clench my fists and hold in a scream. This cannot be! This is ever the same, this pain and suffering will always be.

But there is change, some tiny bits of the aftermath molded into small little stars. Jason's little brother looking at me and saying,

"I want to play baseball and win trophies just like Jason." One of his best friends posting on social media that he wants to make him proud and be the best he can. A young mother reading my blog and holding her son a little tighter because, somehow, I have made a difference by sharing this horrific event.

Some of these stars are shooting stars that have made my world a bit more bearable. Jason's charity, Jason's Propulsion League, has brought the reality of playing baseball to fruition for dozens of young players. Friends, family, and even strangers who have learned of this story are not as quick to judge when they hear of a child who has taken their life. Families hold closer to each other knowing that at any moment their world could change.

Yet, I always come back to the pain and the terrible question, "Why?" Keep holding your babies closer, keep striving to be that better person, keep true to those you love. Take one woman's question of why and make it motivation to shoot for the stars.

JASON FOREVER, FOREVER JASON

* * *

TODAY

Now in January 2013, we had moved yet again, and I found myself in the usual position, drinking wine, sitting in the living room watching some nonsense with the family on TV. This would be the sixth move in three years. The first with the short sale before Jason's passing, the second from needing to find something more affordable, the third because I could not go back to the house where my son died, the fourth caused from that rental getting foreclosed on, the fifth because that owner decided to sell, and now here we were.

I heard the voice, my Jason telling me "Enough," and for the first time I looked up from my sorrow and took inventory of my family. There were my twins, five years old now, wrestling on the couch, their giggles filling the air, their sweet smiles reminding me of how resilient children are, how they can find wonder in anything, and that was invigorating.

From there I glanced at my Brian, the boy who was now sixteen and struggling to find balance with us, yet thriving. He had formed strong bonds with his friends through the loss they all felt when Jason took his life. He was angry of course, but he was handling this better than his mother. It was when I looked at my husband I was shook to the core. He was sitting there, gray and worn, tired to the bone. But he wasn't drowning himself in a drink or out finding a way to escape this horrible reality. He was sitting there, looking back at me like I was going to break.

For two years he carried us all. Through it all he never wavered, he stood tall, finishing up his hazmat degree to try and get us in a better financial position and make captain at the department. He packed up the house those many, many times, called his friends, family, called in favors and moved us, over and over again. He would come home from his shift, no matter how difficult the night had been on calls for fires and accidents, and start cleaning. He would cook, do the laundry, clean the house, do the shopping, hold us, kiss us, take care of us . . . and it was killing him.

"It's time."

I realized my selfishness in not fully trying, in giving up, leaving him to clean up the mess and doing nothing. I had attempted to work a very basic job cashiering, but I could not keep it together and I left after only a few months. It brought a wave of guilt because I knew what I was capable of. I had been a multiproperty owner and millionaire before the age of thirty. Now here I was in a dark, run down, cheap rental, wearing worn-out shirts and using all our money for our children and paying the bills. I had been "training" for this my entire life. From the loss of my father to prison as a very young girl, the abuse of my mother, the bullies, severe ups and downs of financial wealth to financial freedom, beaten by my first husband, drug and alcoholism taking my sister and father, brother gone to cancer. When I began taking inventory of all the hardships and pain, I began to realize I had what everyone talks about in the movies. I had grit.

I sat and took assessment, looked at every piece I was able to face in those moments, and I said, "NO, NO! This is not where my story melts into the forgotten, this is not the fate of my son, and it certainly is NOT what I want for the children and loving husband who have been by my side supporting me through it all."

Your damn right it was time, and the first step I needed to take was finding a way to get us into a house no one could take away. A foundation to build on, to grow with, make part of our family—whatever that was now. Stability, security, roots to grow once again into the tree of our new life.

I noticed, too, as I began to awaken from my long solitude, my blog messages also getting brighter, making connections. My story, the raw telling of it was starting to take root and take on a life of its own.

Chapter 15: Will

Memoir XIII

Will: a deliberate or fixed desire or intention

February 19, 2013

Those of us who have lost a child.

This is dedicated to my fellow mother in the UK. I understand and feel your pain, you are not alone . . .

It's something I fought daily for the first year, wanting to die because I could not handle the pain. The assault on your emotions which starts from the moment you wake, the reality that my child is no longer here. Roller coaster is too kind a word; it's a tornado, a tsunami that hits us every day . . . those of us that have lost a child.

There really are no words to describe what we face, but I write this blog in an effort to share with the world the rawness of these emotions. I write to help others understand we are no different than they are, we have just suffered the unimaginable. I write to help those parents see every thought they have is a normal reaction to their loss. Even the thought of taking their own life.

Appalling as it may sound, the struggle to make it through each hour of every day is horrifying. Imagine, if you will, hitting your hand with a hammer not once, not twice, but several times a day, EVERY DAY. Would you want to wake up and face that on a daily basis? Would you look forward to the brief reprieve that sleep offers? After a year of this, would you want it to end?

This is what we face, and this is one of the reasons the thought of leaving this world enters our mind. Another is the simple desire to see, hear, and hold our child once again. I say simple, yet as a parent it is everything we live for, the essence of our heart and soul.

For me, as time passed, the pain did not subside, but I found ways to distract myself from it. Most importantly, every time I thought of joining my son in Heaven, I would picture his face and the disappointment on it as he would know what I had done. I would also look at my beautiful children I still have and think, "You selfish little worm! How dare you, even for one second, think you could escape pain only to cause it again for them!"

I had to pull myself away from my pity and realize I still have work here, still have little ones that need me. I LOVE them beyond reason, so why would I want them to suffer the loss of their mother? Even at those times when I feel they would be better with someone more stable raising them, they would still suffer the loss and pain I feel now. That is something I will not do: cause them more pain. EVER.

So, as I approach my two-year mark without my beloved Jason, the pain is ever constant, but my will to survive it has grown stronger. I am a strong mother, a proud mother, a mother who wants to see her other children grow and prosper. I still fight the urge to join my Heavenly child, but my resolve to make him proud and beat this tragedy prevails. And in those moments, when I do prevail, I see his smile and know he is here with me.

JASON FOREVER, FOREVER JASON

* * *

TODAY

That is what did it for me, the flick of the switch so to speak. Realizing what I did impacted not only those around me, but those who have been through the same thing. That and the thought of seeing my son again as the broken, lump of a woman I had become. I had to start stepping up and doing something to change my circumstances, not only for my family but for my sanity.

I had a choice to make. Was I going to take the time I had left in this world and become a statistic, marred and just running the hamster wheel? Or was I going to be the rock star my son would have wanted his mom to be? I had to start somewhere, had to find the solution to the financial pain so I could start working on the emotional pain.

Yet, how? How was a family to do this with a short sale just two years ago and a bankruptcy discharge but three months ago? Oh, and the tiny fact we didn't have a down payment was kind of important. So I began researching.

I had been listening to the radio, searching the web to find programs, and I called several real estate agents. All of them, every single one, told me they could not help me, that it just couldn't be done. By March of 2013, two months into the search and contacting mortgage lenders, I had found a program that would grant us the down payment and assist with closing costs, and I worked tirelessly to improve our credit scores, and then it happened. My lender called that first part of the worst month of my life, March, and said we did it. We qualified and were completely approved for an extreme extenuating circumstance loan and we could move forward. The underwriters all agreed the extremes of our conditions, from the time of pay cuts and two of our children being special needs to the extreme emotional stress of losing our son to suicide, they were giving us a chance. At the time I was told this had been the only one they had ever seen approved. I had beat all the odds.

But we would still need some assistance with closing, and again, no real estate agent would help us because they had never seen an extenuating circumstance loan actually close and go through, or they were not willing to contribute toward our closing costs as I had heard a few agents did for first responders.

Once again, I took assessment and said, "NO." I had gotten us this far, I would take us the rest of the way. I started looking up real estate schools and saw I could get through it in two weeks, but I would have to use what little funds we had in savings to pay for the school and licensing. The last few hundred dollars in our account, and I had to do it quick. My husband could not continue to push himself more, my kids needed a brighter and healthier environment, and I NEEDED a purpose.

Ironically, I raced through school and completed all the classes in eighteen days, going in between my husband's shifts at the fire station. With the desperate thrust of a person being stranded in the desert, I crammed for the test and passed the first time, officially becoming licensed the day before the second anniversary of my son's death. By the end of March 2013 I had my real estate license in hand and was searching for a home, and nothing was going to stop me.

Chapter 16: Angel

Memoir XIV

Angel: a spiritual being believed to act as an attendant, agent, or messenger of God.

April 6, 2013

Angel in the Outfield

Last month was a very difficult month. Two years without my Jason. Like so many other parents who have lost their child, we wonder when the pain will ease and WHEN the "time will heal" is supposed to kick in. I suppose we wonder endlessly why and how we continue forward.

Today I was reminded moving forward is only possible because of what I do to honor my son. I attended my second Opening Day ceremony for the league I was able to support in memory of Jason. Clarendon Little League received $2,300.00 for registration fees and over $5,000.00 of new and gently used equipment through my beautiful little charity, Jason's Propulsion League. Something

I couldn't do without those who have supported us along the way.

As my husband and I arrived at the field, we couldn't help but feel cheated as we had to be here without him. Then, as we looked around at all the happy faces, the parents and siblings taking part in their child's celebration, we realized he was here. He was here because our efforts in raising funds and equipment allowed these children the opportunity to play. He was here because his spirit drove others to support our cause and work hard for these children. He was here because he is never far from me.

As I looked out onto the field, I was suddenly taken aback. Out on the fence, the largest of all the signs, was a special tribute to my boy, a banner with his charity name and his jersey number, thirteen. The tears flowed. I was so honored! As the parade began they made the announcement that we had helped dozens of children play this year, and I would be throwing out the first pitch!

As I walked to the mound, I closed my eyes and pictured my boy at the last game I watched him pitch, just two days before he left us. Wearing the same jersey and cap, using his glove, I looked straight down the line, aiming for the catcher's glove . . . STRIKE!

He was there, he was there, my Angel in the Outfield, he was there! Shortly after, we gathered our things and left for home. In the car I looked down at the beautiful plaque the league had presented to me, and I was struck with the realization I will hold it close forever.

Today, through me, my Jason threw his signature fastball, and today, through me, my Jason received another trophy to add to his collection. I miss you, my boy, but I know you are here!

JASON FOREVER, FOREVER JASON

* * *

Today

That was another pivotal moment, and by no coincidence when I needed it most. Opening Day ceremonies at another new inner city league was coming up, and I wore Jason's last baseball jersey with the number thirteen. It was an incredible feeling at the ceremonies that day, old-school style with families grilling, conversing, and smiles everywhere.

Our contributions helped out every kid there either with equipment or money. That throw . . . I felt it, felt his energy—or at least his working through me—and it showed me angels can live here on Earth, through us, those that love them. We can endeavor to be that exemplary person, that one who lives in a space of service and giving.

I had finished real estate school, but just because you have gone to school does not mean you know what you are doing or how to get a buyer or even how to get started. Then there was the issue of a marketing budget—yeah, let me just slip that check in the mail. So I studied, followed what other agents were doing, and did have one buyer at least—myself.

When I actually found a home we could afford that was close to the twins school and was willing to accept our offer using a grant and extenuating circumstances loan, I experienced the first taste of hope. Now, hope is not one of my favorite words, it indicates a desire, a dream, if you will, and it can waver. Yet, in that moment, that feeling breaking through the crust of my pain was exhilarating.

Then it happened, pushing through what seemed like mountains of paperwork to prove our circumstances truly had horrific consequences on our finances; not only that, but we also had to show we had turned it around, that we could move forward and forge a better life and pay this mortgage. It was no easy feat, and I counted the emails that went back and forth between the lender and I during the process; over four hundred of them and countless paperwork.

I did it. I had taken an impossible situation and officially closed on OUR home on June 1, 2013, just two months from getting licensed and with no more than $1200 out of our pocket. That day changed the forward path of my life beyond anything I could have imagined and put me on a trajectory of achieving a legacy I never thought I would see again.

I had no idea at the time what life had in store for me. What I did know was what happened when I gave those keys to my husband, and the reaction he had next as he turned the key to open the door of HIS house. As we walked inside this well-loved and in-much-need-of-updating home, I consciously watched them all: the twins running in circles in the family room, giggling at all the space and natural light; Brian, now sixteen, already planning where to soundproof his room so he can write music; and my husband . . . it was looking over at him that caused a bubble to form within, a bubble that had no better description than joy.

I had given him his pride back, his strength, his ability to protect and to keep his family safe. A FOUNDATION.

In that moment, I felt it again for the first time since losing Jason—JOY. Like tiny little bubbles that kiss your face. I felt it. I felt it to my core, awakening my broken and battered soul, and I realized I HAD DONE THIS. I had been able to create my own joy through sheer will and determination to change my family's life. I BELIEVED in myself.

Real estate is not buying and selling houses, it is the ability to give a family a gift, a new chapter, a new beginning, security, and joy. I had found my purpose, and I jumped in with everything I had. I was going to give this to others, the ones who didn't think they ever could, or that no one would take on. I was going to rebate my commission as much as I could to help with closing costs, to walk that line with them and to fight to get that home for them. Yet, I had no funds to market myself, I could not join a team because of the time in the office required, and I had four therapies a week with my autistic son. How the hell was I going to compete with the well-established agents who dominated out there?

Honestly, I said to myself, fuck it, I am not going to compete, I am just going to be exactly who I am because I don't have to change to be the change. I manifested change for my family and fought for it, blood, sweat, tears, whatever it took, and I did not back down, I did not give up. That's what I had to offer: an agent who would FIGHT for those families and never give up.

I had been raised in the world of corporate negotiations, and even though my father had his issues, his negotiation skills were off the charts, and I had taken note. I was a natural researcher, and he had also taught me the art of investigation. What did that make me? Tenacious is what it made me. Tenacity with a heart.

Thus was born Tenacious T.

I had my brand and my slogan: Through homeownership, I help families who have been through hardships to start a new chapter. I took to social media, to realtor home tours, to events, and introduced myself as "Hi, my name is Kimberly Tocco, they call me Tenacious T."

I would get odd looks, rolling eyes, and even double takes, but they definitely remembered me, and that was my only goal. Remember who I am and why I am in this. It was lonely. Most professionals in the industry loved my idea of a giving back platform, but they did not see it as sustainable. They saw it as a discount program and a gimmick to get clients.

In the meantime, we were still struggling financially, so giving back half of what I was making was extremely stressful. I wasn't going to alter my vision, though. I had to find a way to make it work, to build a business on giving back. I tried joining small teams, but again, they had taken their cut after I had already given back to my client, along with the broker cut, and that left me with very little.

I also learned "teams" were not necessarily there to help you build your business and brand, you were there to help them build theirs. I had to go solo, independent, and find a broker who supported my giving back—not just supported it, but saw the vision of what I was trying to do, which was build community in the industry. Yet, who was I? A girl with a GED and no marketing experience outside of a brief stint in movies and commercials years ago.

Then I heard it again, the voice in my head, which let out a small whisper: "Stick with it, keep going."

I had been weeping again, going through some of Jason's things, trying to find purpose and meaning in all of it, trying to find anything to get me through these episodes of hopelessness a parent feels when they have lost a child to suicide, and trying to build a business.

Here I was, just a few months into one of the most difficult careers to sustain, in a city with the highest concentration of real estate agents per capita, with nothing but a foundation of suicide to build it on. Yet this is not my foundation, this is Jason's, and I cannot let him go down like that. I cannot sit here and watch all his brightness, his laughter and light, be remembered as just that, a boy who took his life and became a statistic.

THAT IS NOT WHO HE WAS.

For every moment I would have held him, fed him, taught him, loved him, and cherished him, I will pour into this business. For every time I tell myself I can't, I will look in the mirror and tell HIM I can. With every ounce of my being, my Jason will be remembered as a LIFE CHANGER.

Because his mother is going to be wildly successful through building a business based on giving back and solidifying herself in the social media world and making a name in the real estate game. Then I could bring his purpose to life, write his book, tell his tale through my eyes, and turn his foundation of suicide into a platform to SAVE lives.

As I watched the many motivational videos and famous catalysts of inspiration, they all had one thing in common: they had stuck with it and made their fortunes so they could tell their stories. They proved themselves as successful, and others paid attention. I HAD to succeed, I HAD to show through sheer determination and grit I could overcome my circumstances.

"Stick with it, keep going."

I remembered the letter he wrote about baseball, at the time tucked in my desk. I searched for it and pulled it from the drawer.

BASEBALL

One of the most amazing games I have ever played was last year on my White Sox team. In the last inning, the score was tied one to one. I had pitched a pretty good game. I was up to bat, bases loaded, two outs, I have two strikes, last pitch comes right down the middle. I swing, I felt the connection of the bat, the ball flew out over the fence and I had hit my first homer of the game. We beat them five to one. That was one of the most amazing games I have ever played.

I laid the paper down and let it all go. The tears flowed as I felt how tired I had become, like a daily battle that just kept going. How is it my efforts to build a business on giving back would be fought against? To build community where we all just shared our secrets and lifted each other up would fall on deaf ears? I felt the embers of anger rise again, frustration, and defeat. Then I walked over, picked up one of his bats, and began to swing. I swung it like he did in that game.

I remember it so well.

He was standing there, his entire team watching him. This was the championship, and he stared that ball down in the final pitch and it flew over the fence.

My son was a champion, and it's the championship mentality I needed to adopt. I had made the connection, and nothing was going to stop me. My boy needed me, and this was going to be my home run.

I thought of that paper, that determination, that willpower he had in those few minutes at twelve years old, and I knew I could do this.

I had his wings, and we were going to fly.

By the end of that year, 2013, I had made Rookie of the Year at RE/MAX Excalibur. Year two I doubled my sales, qualified and completed Leadership Academy XIII, all while fighting the industry on my views on giving back and building my brand 100 percent on my own through sheer will and determination.

I used my creativity and love for movies along with speaking my truth and actually giving a shit. Brokerages would sit me down and tell me to build my wealth first and give back later, that I would never succeed by giving it all away first. They also made it clear if I continued to give back, they would need to raise the fees, as they were making less from it as well.

I would tell them to sit down at the signing table with my clients and tell them that. Tell that family who is finally going to be homeowners or the family that is getting a fresh start, "Hey, you know what? I will send you a gift card in like five years when I am rolling in the dough. I can't give you any of this commission right know, I am going to keep it."

I was not going to listen to them. I just kept giving back because that's why I was doing this. I switched brokerage offices and found some who had no problem with what I did and were kind. Yet, the community in the office was competitive and the culture, though they did try, was not 100 percent from the heart. It was still "Each man for himself," so to speak.

I started mentoring new agents as I excelled in sales, breaking records for selling at top dollar and buyers closing with instant equity because I had negotiated the prices down. I worked to make the experience for all my clients and agents something they would never forget—the feeling I had when I gave those keys to my husband. JOY had become currency and I wanted to give it to everyone.

Also, as it turned out, my marketing and negotiating skills were something to be reckoned with and agents wanted to learn what I was doing.

No one was really utilizing the creative platform or doing what I was on the philanthropic side, and they certainly were not taking the risks with the videos and ads I was making. Good or bad, like that first few months in real estate, people were remembering my name, hearing the words "Tenacious T" trickling in everywhere. I worked tirelessly thinking up little things that would make me stand out. Including my children in my ads and just showing them my passion for what I was doing. Bringing humor and fun back into the scene.

Then it started to really happen. The giveback community started noticing me, and I began to find others giving back in their own ways, and my business flourished, and collaborations were made.

I broke into the six figures even with my giving back. By year three, I was a sledgehammer, a machine never missing a close, confining my streak on breaking records and adding in pro bono work. We were taking elaborate trips again; I could buy whatever food my kids wanted. I was winning awards, receiving invites, doubling my sales, and helping families into the hundreds now.

March 22, 2018, I launched a video which began to change the trajectory of my career and path. His anniversary month, March, five years into my real estate career and seven years from the last moments I had with my son, I was going to have my first six-figure month. All on my own, a month with eleven transactions and clearing just over one hundred thousand dollars in thirty days. I had done it, succeeded, and I finally understood the true meaning of "When you want to succeed as bad as you want to breathe, then you'll be successful," which was said by Eric Thomas, an author and motivational speaker.

I did not want to breathe, I wanted to succeed.

And once again, I heard his voice.

"It's time, Mom, time to tell my story."

Yes, that never stopped for me, not for any of us who have lost a child. We NEVER stop thinking of them, crying for them, looking for them in everything we do. I could hear him. He was right, I had done it. Like that moment when my husband had turned the key and stepped into our home, with a foundation under his feet that no one could take from him, it hit me like that. It was time to finish the book . . . his book. But I needed one more thing. I needed national exposure about my story: who I was, what I had been through, what I had achieved, and why I was writing this book.

Anyone can write a book, but you need to inspire people, show them not only what you overcame but how you were able to do it. I had achieved the financial success, at least the beginnings of the abundance that was starting to come in. I had joined a brokerage innovative in its structure and owned by agents. They were all about building community and culture; they shared their secrets and we helped each other, mentoring, master minds globally through a cloud-based office. They loved my giving and probing work, and it was the perfect fit. They "saw" me. Now I had to accomplish something rare few do, and it had to be authentic, not paid for.

I set my goals on television and HGTV. If I could get just one episode on a well-known show—just ONE—I could propel that and use it for good. I posted a video about my loss, my journey, my new pro bono piece for families that have lost a child, and my success, and within a few months a casting director sent me an email.

A new show for the network, for HGTV, House Hunters style, only about pools. They wanted this to be real, not choreographed, the real deal. A family who moved here for opportunity and to have the famous Arizona-style backyard. They had seen a few of my videos, and they thought I would be good on film.

Did I have a family that matched what they were looking for?

You bet I did. Of course I did. By now I understood some things happen for a reason, and I had been working with the most wonderful family. Our interview sessions went all the way up the ladder, and the call came. They were coming out the last four days of September and everyone needed to be on board and ready to film all day.

That in itself was a feat, both parents being physicians and three young boys in school, but we made it work and everything went off without a hitch. During that time, I had connected with a family friend, who was creating my new fifteen-year anniversary ring for Peter and I's vow renewal. I was taking my whole family to Hawaii, a place Jason loved, to renew our vows in the oldest church on the Big Island.

When Pete and I married we had exchanged family medallions with Brian and Jason to give them a part in the ceremony. We wanted that again, and the jeweler who had created the ring also had started a movement with what he called the Intention Stick: a tube, if you will, engraved with the tree of life and a space inside you could place one to three of the twenty-two words of intention the necklace came with, vowing to live by the intention of those words and share your story and intention every day in some way. It is called The Tree of Life Movement.

We gave those to the twins and Brian at the renewal, and as we finished up with the film crew, I shared the necklace with them. I wanted to mark the event I knew would catapult my story and help it spread. To live with intention and purpose, and change lives one story at a time.

It became a gift I would share many times along the way. I also learned the maker of the necklace happened to be living in the same house my Jason had visited many, many times in his life: his biological grandparents' home.

What are the odds of that?

And yes, that was a huge nudge to share my intention and spread the message. Jason wanted me to share OUR story, how we overcame this together and encourage others to do the same.

The following twelve months moved hard and fast. Like a locomotive that comes up quickly and you have to start running as fast as you can if you ever think you will have the opportunity to grab the rail and jump on.

I was running. Running with every fiber of my being, and my body was starting to shut down. I worked to the point of exhaustion every day, but I could not stop. I was almost there.

We filmed the show, and it would launch in eight months IF the network liked the final product. I had found a brokerage and a mentor who believed in me and embraced my giving back. I was mentoring five agents and running the real estate side. I had been actively speaking out about suicide while still running my real estate company.

I needed to start a podcast, I needed to design a website, I needed to slow down, but I didn't know how or who to turn to.

I had gotten mono, reoccurring esteem bar inflammation, Valley Fever, parvo virus, and pertussis all in a twelve-month time, and also iron transfusions due to anemia.

I was in pain and still working up to sixty hours a week.

I couldn't maintain this pace, and I was losing steam. Drive will do that to you, and the window was open, this was my shot—this was Jason's shot. This was OUR TIME.

That's when three very important people came into my life.

One was a hugely successful coach, author, and entrepreneur whose kindness in taking me on confirmed my story would touch people. He changed my entire perception of what a leader really is. A leader listens, comes up with solutions, and lifts up the spirit by helping others because they have done it. A leader helps one to uncover what they had inside themselves all along.

He taught me life lessons become the stories which illustrate struggles and triumphs, and you build on that. You believe in people and the process, take off some of your hats others can handle, and lift the weight off your shoulders so you can be free to develop more of the talents you excel in.

Another was a mentor and the man who connected me with the greatest brokerage of all time and showed me a way to make money outside of the real estate hustle. Someone who believed in everything I was doing, and we lifted each other up. His guidance in pain freedom also lead me to seek the path of inner wisdom and peace through breathwork, grounding, and the cold. In the cold, for the first time, I truly felt how I had control of my mind.

The third gave me answers through showing me how to turn into myself and heal what was wrong.

That third person was me. I had finally figured out who I was again, and I was a seeker of joy and a guide to show others how I found it again.

When I looked in the mirror now, I saw a stunning, beautiful woman who exuded strength and love at the same time. She also looked back at me and was proud. For the very first time in my life I had no doubt or hesitation of what I was building, and the woman looking back at me was worthy of the task.

"Why me?" turned into "Why not me?"

To further solidify now was the time, Jason also gave me a typewriter. I had been hesitating again on completing his book, not sure it would truly make a difference. I had just closed on an investment deal for a client who lived in California, and out of the blue he said, "You know I was in my attic the other day and came across my aunt's old typewriter. I know you said you had a book you were completing, and I thought I would give it to you."

I love antiques, and, yes, of course I would take the typewriter. Very old, and it had been sitting in his attic, a man I didn't know at all with the exception of being a co-agent on a deal with an agent I had been mentoring. I took it from him and brought it home, setting it under Jason's collage of pictures in my office. It sat there for a couple of days until I sat down to try and write my book again. I walked over to it as it had an old, worn leather cover on it, and I was curious to read what had been stamped into the leather those many, many years ago. It was a Remington, and just below the name, a number thirteen. Jason once again, like the Tootsie Roll wrapper falling from the ice machine, he was showing me what to do.

IT WAS TIME.

I had success, recognition, and momentum, yet I was still running at an impossible speed. I wanted this legacy now. I had envisioned it, built it, designed the path, and it had all come together. I looked to my left and saw I was gaining speed and moving faster than the train.

Now was the time to jump. Now was the time to fly.

Chapter 17: Tenacious Angel

Memoir XV

Tenacious Angel: a person of exemplary conduct or virtue . . . in a leather jacket

November 5, 2019

Letter to my son.

Oh, my dear boy, how do I put into words what you already know? It has been three-thousand-one-hundred and fifty days since you took your life.

Even as I write this, I weep.

You are gone from this world but never from my heart.

What I would not give . . .

Yet, that is not where we are now, is it, my boy? We are far from the dark shadows of grief and the pain it carried on its back. I took what you taught me so early on in your short stint here

with me, with us, with the handful of those who knew you. Your enthusiasm for helping a friend, a brother, the light and laughter you brought into a room. I nurtured that everyday within me so I could once again find that joy in order to honor you.

You woke me from a very deep sleep, one that very few can climb out of. Something very unique happens when someone has been pummeled and beat over and over again, stepped on and ground into the black dirt.

It seems the world is laughing while life is slaughtering you.

When you can no longer take being skinned alive each and every day, suddenly you realize you have a choice. You are faced with obliteration or rebirth. Literally a crossroads. You have to choose.

And I choose you, my son. I CHOOSE you.

The moment I gave over to that, I knew what they meant by the old saying "An angel here on Earth."

In order to honor you I had to be worthy of you, and that meant setting my heart to a purpose of serving and giving, allowing myself to feel everything and not be ashamed of it, which developed into understanding and recognizing when I see that pain in others. Then reaching out to those "others" and connecting with your story—our story—to lift them up and show them what happens when you choose life.

That choice has a ripple effect, just as your death had a ripple effect. I do not know why—I can speculate what your reasons were in that moment, but your life is not suicide. Your life is the smile on your brother's face as he is recording his music, the twins doing a "Jason" pose while on a ride in Disneyland, and Peter when he is watching your favorite football team win.

Your life is your mother, living her dream because of the JOY you so freely gave. I only had you for thirteen years, yet through you I have gained the wisdom of kindness, living in no shame, and serving others as you would have done.

And we have served so many others.

You touched so many lives, Jason, and I know your story has saved lives as well. Your ripple effect is not one of sorrow and tragedy, but one of sheer light, of venerability and strength at the same time.

I took that foundation of suicide and broke through its thick crust. Slowly at first, not really understanding what I was doing.

Then I saw it, that locomotive called OPPORTUNITY rushing by, and I began to walk faster, then jog . . . Now I am running, running hard. The back car is coming up, Son, and I am giving it all I have, as fast as I can, ignoring the pain in my chest. It's your turn now, my boy.

Lend me your wings and let's fly!

Jason Forever, Forever Jason

* * *

OVERCOME Book Two

Tenacious Angels

"When you can fly"

It is not what you go through, it is how you come through it.

~ Tenacious T

* * *

Notes

Chapter 6

1. Merrill, Laurie, and Kerry Fehr-snyder. "Speaking out on Teen Suicide." PressReader.com. *The Arizona Republic*, September 6, 2011. https://www.pressreader.com/usa/the-arizona-republic/20110906/282832187826479.

About the Author

Kimberly Tocco, solutionist, implementor, realtor extraordinaire, and suicide eradicator, continues her efforts to change lives from her beloved home in the Valley of the Sun. Going on nineteen years with her husband, a local fire captain, they are still raising their twin boys and are fortunate to have their oldest son living right down the street. Working on her next book, podcast, and changing lives through real estate, her life never has a dull moment.

. . . and she wouldn't want it any other way.

Next up? Why not the red carpet!?

The letter, Jason, glove, ball,
and tootsie roll wrapper.

Jason's final Jersey.

My license plate.

Four boys with their dad.

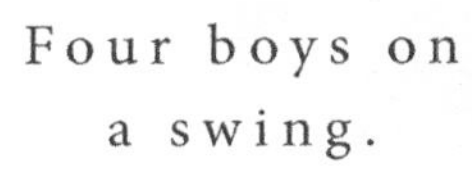

Four boys on a swing.

Brian joining me in real estate.

Philantropsit of the Year Award next to Jason.

The Bat, and XIII tattoo

Peter and Joey, the twins.

Podcasting That Bitchin' Real Estate Show. (From left to right) Debbie Biery, Kristi Culhane, Ashlee Miller, Kimberly Tocco, Angel, Nada Djomehri

In my home office.

Made in United States
North Haven, CT
04 March 2023